"How to Respond to a RFP"

Winning Proposal Writing

First Edition

2010

Cover Artwork by Telesto Inc.,
300 Terry Fox Drive, Suite 100,
Kanata, Ontario
K2K 0E3

www.telesto.ca

Note for Librarians: A cataloguing record for this book is available from Library and Archives Canada at www.collectionscanada.gc.ca/amicus/index-e.html

ISBN 978-0-9812055-6-4

Order this book online at **www.boreal.ca**

How to Respond to an RFP – Winning Proposal Writing and most Boreal titles are available at major online book retailers.

© Copyright 2010 Allan Cutler

All rights reserved. No part of this publication may be reproduced, stored in a retrieval system, or transmitted, in any form or by any means, electronic, mechanical, photocopying, recording, or otherwise, without the written prior permission of the author.

The author and publisher specifically disclaim any responsibility for liability, loss or risk, personal or otherwise, which is incurred as a consequence, directly or indirectly, of the use of any of the contents of this book

Boreal Books
P.O. Box 4693 Postal Stn E,
Ottawa, Ontario
K1S 5H8

Preamble

Winning Proposal Writing, is directed to those who wish to submit bids that give them the best possible chance of coming out a winner.

Winning Proposal Writing has guidelines and suggestions for writing the proposal. It also discusses various elements in complex bidding that affect this writing. A complex Bid/No Bid analysis is discussed.

It focuses on what you must know, and how to write your proposal in a highly-competitive and procedurally-challenging environment.

To be successful, and not waste resources, it is necessary that you understand the unforgiving procurement process, how you may gain competitive advantage, and what you are expected to provide as a successful bidder, in each proposal.

Winning Proposal Writing is the companion book to *Understanding the Bid and Proposal Process*. The two books are strongly linked. *Understanding the Bid and Proposal Process* focuses on the various procurement documents that are in existence and the elements of the customer requirement and customer bid call processes.

Read, heed and succeed. It is said that "you can't win them all." The ultimate achievement is to win your share or more.

Allan Cutler

Table of Contents

PREAMBLE — III

1. RESPONDING TO A RFP — 1
- THE BID DOCUMENTS — 1
- USE OF RFP — 2
- THE RFP PROCESS — 2

2. THE BID/NO-BID DECISION — 5
- THE CHECKLIST — 5
- BID/NO-BID TEMPLATE — 6
- THE BID/NO-BID MATRIX — 9
- NO-BID LETTER – WHAT TO WRITE OR NOT TO WRITE — 12

3. WRITING THE PROPOSAL — 13
- THE METHODOLOGY — 13
- THE INITIAL PROPOSAL MEETING — 14
- EVALUATION CRITERIA — 15
- PROPOSAL PREPARATION: THE TIME ELEMENTS — 16
- FINAL REVIEW — 17
- AMENDMENTS TO RFPS — 18

4. THE RED TEAM — 21
- RED TEAM REVIEW — 21
- COMPOSITION OF RED TEAM — 22
- RESPONDING TO THE RED TEAM REVIEW — 23
- RED TEAM FAILURE — 23
- ERROR AVOIDANCE — 25
- WHEN NOT TO USE A RED TEAM — 26
- TEMPLATES — 27

5. MANAGING BAD RFPS — 29

6. PROPOSAL RESPONSE – ELEMENTS — 33
- EXECUTIVE SUMMARY — 34
- STAFFING PLAN — 38
- RESUMES — 40
- CORPORATE EXPERIENCE/PAST PERFORMANCE — 44
- BUSINESS REFERENCES — 47
- TECHNICAL SOLUTION — 48
- MANAGEMENT PLAN — 51
- TRANSITION PLAN — 54

APPENDICES	57
7. BOILERPLATE	**59**
8. GRAPHICS	**61**
9. VERSION CONTROL	**69**
10. EMPTY ASSERTIONS	**71**
11. PRESENTATION OF THE PROPOSAL	**77**
12. PRICING STRATEGIES	**79**
13. PROPRIETARY INFORMATION	**81**
14. THINK LIKE AN EVALUATOR	**83**
15. DEFENSIVE PROPOSAL	**87**
16. BIDDERS' CONFERENCES AND/OR	**89**
SITE VISITS	**89**
17. ORAL PRESENTATIONS	**91**
PREPARATION	92
ROOM/LAYOUT	94
PRESENTERS	95
HANDOUTS	97
BODY LANGUAGE	97
QUESTIONS AND ANSWERS (QS & AS)	100
18. LARGE AND SMALL PROPOSALS:	**103**
THE DIFFERENCE	**103**
LARGE PROPOSAL:	103
SMALL PROPOSAL:	104
19. ALTERNATE PROPOSALS	**105**
20. INCUMBENTS DISADVANTAGE	**107**
21. PROPOSAL PREPARATION: OUTSOURCING	**109**
PERMANENT STAFF	110
OUTSOURCING	110
22. PUBLIC SECTOR VS. PRIVATE INDUSTRY - A COMPARISON	**113**
THE PROCUREMENT PROCESS: IN BRIEF	113
PUBLIC SECTOR	115
PRIVATE INDUSTRY	119

STRATEGIC ALLIANCE	**123**
SUBCONTRACTORS	**125**
BEING A SUBCONTRACTOR	126
APPENDIX A - LETTERS	**129**
NO BID LETTERS	129
APPENDIX B THE TOP TEN	**131**
THE TOP 10 REVIEWING A RFP	131
THE TOP TEN WHEN PREPARING A PROPOSAL DON'T…	132
THE TOP TEN WHAT EVALUATORS WANT	133
THE TOP TEN MAJOR MISTAKES IN PREPARING A PROPOSAL	134
APPENDIX C CASE STUDY	**139**
APPENDIX D – TEMPLATE FOR PROPOSAL PREPARATION	**169**
EXAMPLE 1	169
EXAMPLE 2	171
APPENDIX E	**175**
PROFESSIONAL RESUME – ALLAN CUTLER	**175**

1. Responding to a RFP

The Bid Documents

There are three main bidding tools that all use essentially the same process and methodology – Request for Proposal (RFP), Request for Standing Offer (RFSO) and Request for Supply Arrangement (RFSA). The main difference from a bidder's perspective is how they are used once a "winner" is determined.

The Request for Proposal (RFP) is used for large dollar value requirements when the requirements need interpretation and are not easily defined. Bidders submit their proposal and the result is a contract.

Request for Standing Offer (RFSO) is used for repetitive competitive purchases where the requirement of the elements of the services can be defined. The bidder submits an offer that conforms to the requirements. The resulting document authorizes this offer. A contract will be formed only when there is an actual need and through a call-up (acceptance of the offer) which is issued against the Standing Offer.

Request for Supply Arrangement (RFSA) is the middle ground between RFPs and RFSOs. It is used for large dollar value repetitive competitive purchases where the requirements can only be defined generally and there is no guarantee of usage. The most common usage is to create a pre-qualified list of suppliers. When there is a requirement, only these preselected suppliers may be given an opportunity to compete for the requirement. This shortens the procurement processing time.

While the procurement process is similar for all three bidding tools, the end result has important implications for the successful firm. Knowing the difference between the above bid documents helps you understand the risk associated with the respective bid. Understanding this also helps in determining whether the costs of submitting a proposal are reasonable and justifiable.

Use of RFP

Each bid is unique, be it simple or complicated and involves numerous stages – presentations, site visits, bidders' conferences, demonstrations, etc. However, the same procurement process and methodology is used for Request for Proposals (RFP), Request for Standing Offer (RFSO) or Request for Supply Arrangement (RFSA).

The term Request for Proposal is best known and often used as a generic expression when people refer to complex bids. Therefore, throughout this book, Request for Proposal (RFP) has been employed in its generic sense and refers to RFPs, RFSOs or RFSAs.

The RFP Process

RFPs require people to think about their requirements and are issued by an organization for a specific project or service. They may or may not be able to provide sufficient details about what a proposal should cover but the process requires them to make an effort to define their needs.

Within the RFP there is a statement of work (requirements definition), deliverables (end result), terms and conditions, completion time frame, the evaluation criteria, method of evaluation and the closing date (or expiry date) of the RFP.

A RFP is a bid issued by a customer asking firms to provide a specific project or service. RFPs generally inform the bidder regarding how to prepare and submit a proposal. The detailed evaluation criteria are designed to allow the customer's evaluators to compare bids.

A statement is normally made that bids will not be compared and that each bid stands alone. Interesting, what often happens is that although each bid is evaluated separately against the evaluation criteria, once the results have been determined the total scores obtained on each bid will be compared. This is considered a comparison of scores, not a comparison of bids. It helps the process of selecting the best proposal and eliminates favouritism in the awarding of the resulting contract.

Also factored into the evaluation are the financial bids that accompany the technical bids. The result is the final evaluation may be done on price or a blend of quality and price with the best value (as defined) being awarded the contract. There are a number of different methods of blending the evaluation of the written proposal (technical bid) and the financial proposal.

Large RFPs are normally extremely complex and can be for multiple locations and multiple users of the service even when only one contract is being issued. For most firms the cost of preparing a proposal is very expensive once you factor in the cost of the time spent on analyzing the RFP, developing and preparing the proposal, and the production costs. As a rough estimate, you should plan on spending 1 to 1 ½ % for the value of the resulting contract for large contracts in the preparation. For small contracts this can be increased up to 5%.

Public procurement is very structured. Governments and bureaucrats are concerned with public accountability, transparency, integrity and the appearance of fairness. Bids are subject to audit and every company has the ability to complain about the procurement to the manager, Minister, Mayor, or other elected officials. Private industry RFPs have a different accountability – to a shareholder and firms are not normally in a position to challenge the results of a bid.

Although private industry does not have to follow the same rules, as the company grows in size, the procurement practices evolve closer to the public sector.

2. The Bid/No-Bid Decision

The Checklist

This is one of the most important decisions that a firm can make. The cost of bidding on complex requirements is very expensive. Continued unsuccessful bidding becomes very costly.

You probably should not bid unless you have at least a one in four chance of winning. The question becomes, "How do we determine whether we should bid or not?"

For simple requirements, you can construct a simple checklist to give some guidance. This is simply a list of questions that you use for all RFPs, listing the major items of importance to your firm in bidding. The checklist is straightforward. You simply create a checkmark to the right for each item that is favourable. If you are not certain, then you leave it blank. Place an "X" in every spot that is negative.

The end product is a series of answers that have been checked off. From this list, you then make a decision on whether you should proceed or not.

The question at the top of most checklists is, "Are we qualified to do the job?" If you place an "X" on the first question, "Are we qualified to do the job?" then stop. There is no point in proceeding further if the answer is "No".

It should be pointed out that this decision is a simple one. It does not consider the situation where you may be qualified to do the job in association with another firm. It considers only whether you should even consider bidding.

Bid/No-Bid Template

For somewhat more complex requirements a template could be used. The difference is that each answer is scored on a scale (eg. 1 to 5). The above question, "Are we qualified to do the job?" may produce a score of 3 or 4 out of 5. Unlike the checklist, in this case you are rating the degree of ability. Therefore, the consideration of working in association with another firm is valid. You are almost certain that you can do the job but may need to find a specialist subcontractor. Each answer is scored separately. At the end, you total all the scores to make your assessment.

For example if the total marks available total 100, you may assess as follows:
0 - 50   No Bid
51 – 69   Further Analysis required
70 – 100   Bid.

The template works under a simple premise. It enables you to balance important factors and helps to guide the decision making process. A sample template with typical results is produced below. Please note that all decisions are scored from 1 to 5. The total of all scores are added together to give guidance on making a decision. The template is a tool to aid in making a decision. It does not replace the need to make a judgment call after considering the score totals and other information.

The total score may indicate that you should bid but you may decide not to. Conversely, the total score may indicate that you should not bid but you may decide to bid anyway. Though guided by the revelations provided by the templates results, in the end your decision is almost always affected by subjective reasoning.

The Bid/No-Bid Decision

In the case below, each criteria has a weight assigned to it. This allows for a more detailed assessment.

For ease of use, the evaluation has been assessed out of a total mark of 100. As already stated, generally for a total resulting in 50 or less the decision is No Bid. For a score resulting in 70 or more, the decision is generally Bid. Between these two ranges further analysis and reasoning is needed.

To further help focus the evaluation, the sample template below is divided into four separate groups – The Customer, The Market, The Bid and The Firm.

Bid/No-Bid Decision Template

Score Scale: 1 - 5

1 represents the most negative and unfavourable response and 5 represents the most favourable response.

A. The Customer

Criteria	Score
1. How well do we know the customer?	5
2. How well does the customer know us?	4
3. Will the evaluators favour our firm?	4
4. Do we know who is ultimately going to OK the recommended bid?	3
5. Are we all in agreement that we know what they want?	4
Subtotal (out of 25)	20

How to Respond to a RFP
Winning Proposal Writing

B. The Market

Criteria	Score
6. How well do we know the business the customer is in?	5
7. How well are we known in the business?	2
8. Is this our core business?	2
9. Do we know how many competitors are bidding, and who they are?	5
10. Would winning the bid present future opportunities for other work?	4
Subtotal (out of 25)	18

C. The Bid

Criteria	Score
11. Do we have enough time to get our proposal ready	4
12. Is the project approved and funded?	5
13. Does the requirement have a high risk of failure?	1
14. Is the RFP complex (as opposed to easy to understand)	3
15. Are the evaluation criteria fair and reasonable?	5
16. Are there difficulties with the Statement of Work/Requirements	4
Subtotal (out of 30)	22

D. Our Firm

Criteria	Score
17. Are we qualified to do the job?	2
18. Do we have the resources to do the proposal?	2
19. Can we accept the contract Terms and Conditions??	5
20. Can we manage the cash flow situation that would result?	5
Subtotal (out of 20)	14

Total = A + B + C + D = 20 + 18 + 22 + 14 = 74

The total score was 74 out of 100. Based on the grid above, this indicates that the firm should bid.

Judgment must now be exercised. When making the final decision a few warning signs are apparent. Criteria 17 and 18 may present a critical problem as resources are not available. Also, in criteria 13, it was indicated that the project has a very high risk of failure.

The Bid/No-Bid Matrix

The Bid/No-Bid Matrix is designed for complex requirements and difficult decisions. The Checklist is simply a list that you analyze. The Template is more advanced than the Checklist but all the questions are rated the same value. With the Bid/No-Bid Matrix, each question has its own value. The answers to some questions are more important than the answers to others.

The weights represent the degree of importance attached to a criteria by your firm and should be standard for all RFPs analyzed. This is where you factor in your judgment regarding the decision. This means that for each question raised you don't need an absolute yes or no regarding the Bid/No-Bid decision.

In the following example, although the Bid/No-Bid factor used was three (3), it could be any number that suits your firm. The total marks available are 27 x 3 which equals 81. To verify the calculations are correct add the Total Bid (52) to the Total No-Bid (29). 52 + 29 also equals 81.

You must always keep in mind that the Bid/No-Bid matrix will never give you a final decision. It gives you an indication. Your judgment must always be used although you should have a better guide.

Reviewing the example also gives you a good reason for bidding as the service was the core business (criteria 3). However, the analysis also revealed that you might not be able to get the proposal prepared on time (criteria 5) and there are problems with the Statement of Work (criteria 7). You have to decide if these are correctable in time or are acceptable risks.

As a final word of caution, it may be that the weights you applied need to be reconsidered and you are inadvertently biasing the outcome. You must double check your calculations and each decision to ensure that the score was correct.

The Bid/No-Bid Decision

Bid/No Bid Matrix

Criteria	Weight	Bid	No Bid	Total Bid	Total No Bid
1. How well do we know the customer?	1	2	1	2	1
2. How well do we know the business?	3	1	2	3	6
3. Is this our core business?	5	3	0	15	0
4. Would winning present other opportunities for work?	2	0	3	0	6
5. Do we have enough time to prepare our bid?	4	2	1	8	4
6. Are the evaluation criteria fair and reasonable?	4	3	0	12	0
7. Are there difficulties with the Statement of Work?	3	1	2	3	6
8. Can we accept the Terms and Conditions?	2	3	0	6	0
9. Can we manage the cash flow situation that would result?	3	1	2	3	6
Totals	27	15	12	**52**	**29**

It would appear to indicate that you should bid. However, if you put this into a percentage, 52/81 = 64%, it becomes much more understandable and more open to examination.

No-Bid Letter – What to write or not to write

If you have reviewed the RFP and decided not to bid, it is always recommended that you send a letter regard your decision.

The key is to be tactful. You don't want to say, "I didn't bother bidding since the criteria were too stringent." The last thing that you want is to eliminate future opportunities to bid and to close doors. The letter should say that although you could not bid this time, you may be able to the next time.

There may be other reasons why you don't want to do business with that client such as a lack of trust, extremely slow payment or personality clashes. Never "cut your own throat" by being that direct. Silence is not lying and being tactful leaves future opportunities open. Circumstances may change at the client level such as a new owner or a change of personnel.

Positive writing is not difficult. Instead of saying, "We don't want to bid because…" you might say, "The reasons that have made it difficult to develop a proposal at this time are unavoidable and they are …" By rewriting the sentence as suggested you avoid using a negative statement. The second sentence expresses a negative but by using "unavoidable" you indicate that there was a reason for the difficulty and by stating "at this time" you indicate that the difficulty can be overcome in the future.

Examples of Bid/No-Bid letters are in Appendix A

3. Writing the Proposal

The Methodology

Competitive proposal writing is a matter of being methodical. Always keep in mind that the evaluator's don't read, they evaluate for points. They are looking for complete information. The KISS principle (Keep it Simple Stupid) applies to writing a proposal.

There is no excuse for writer's block if you know the subject matter that you are bidding on. Don't worry about a beginning or an end. Don't worry about the writing style or using the exact words. Write an overview about the content that the evaluation has demanded and the words will come.

This will give you a clear focus. You can then go back and write in the supporting details. Finally, you can go back and look at the writing and rewrite for polish. In this way you will develop a good proposal.

Some RFPs will set a page limit on the proposal and some won't. Some RFPs will tell you the format/layout to use and some won't. Some RFPs will tell you what evaluation criteria and process the customer will follow and some won't. If there are instructions, follow them. If there are no instructions, write the length necessary to answer the evaluation criteria. In other words give your customer what they want.

Writing a proposal is a process and should be treated as such. It is a process that is logically defined. Creating and following checklists for each step will ensure that nothing is omitted. You will also discover that writing the proposal becomes quicker as you develop boilerplates and examples of the various elements (such as strategic planning) that you have done before.

The Initial Proposal Meeting

On large bids, there is often an initial meeting of the Proposal Team and the Red Team. The main purpose of this meeting is to ensure that all members of both Teams understand their roles.

At the same time, this is a good meeting to address some critical basic requirements needed for the preparation of all sections. For example:
- All sections should be written in a positive tone, not negative
- Page layout will be constant and done by the graphics department (if you have one).
- All header/footers will be consistent.
- Sections will be subject to change as amendments to the RFP are issued.
- Questions regarding sections need to be addressed quickly and given to the Proposal Manager.

It is also helpful to remind the Teams that the evaluation is done on both the mandatory and rated requirements.
1. You must pass the mandatory requirement or the bid is lost.
2. To win the contract, you must obtain the best score based on the rated requirements. Watch carefully for rated requirements which mandate that you must obtain a minimum number of points. (eg. …must obtain at least 80 points to qualify.)
3. And – you must obtain the best possible score based on price and quality.

A good point to stress is that while graphs make information easier to digest and understand, they must also answer the question "Why are they there?" Graphs have to have a reason for being in the proposal. Graphs, for the sake of having graphs, are pointless and detract from your presentation.

Finally, you must point out that all boilerplate material has to be reviewed and updated to ensure that old references to previous bids are removed and that the material is up to date.

Evaluation Criteria

This is the critical part of the bid document from the bidder's perspective when writing the proposal. It is how your proposal will be evaluated and subsequently compared with proposals from other bidders.

The evaluation should be designed to bring objectivity to subjectivity. Every proposal by a bidder for a service is written subjectively. The customer's goal is to develop a fair evaluation mechanism that gives all firms an opportunity to prove their service can do the job and should be chosen. Evaluation criteria are divided into two parts – mandatory and rated.

Mandatory Evaluation Criteria

Mandatory evaluation criteria are supposed to be the minimum requirements necessary for a bid to be considered. They appear on their own and use the words "must", "shall" and "will" in the descriptive narrative.

Generally, mandatory conditions are also considered to be the terms and conditions that are spelled out and conforming to all elements of the Statement of Work. Although it may not be written clearly in the evaluation section, there is usually a statement to the effect, "...the bidder must conform to all the terms and conditions contained herein..." This is something that you must be careful about. Without realizing the consequences, some firms make small changes to these clauses with the result that their bids are judged "non-responsive" and not considered further.

Rated Evaluation Criteria:

The rated evaluation criteria take many forms. They describe minimum requirements that a firm must meet to be considered a 'responsive" bidder. It is important to always try and exceed the minimum. The more points that you earn from your proposal, the better are the odds of your winning the contract.

As stated previously, some rated requirements mandate that you obtain a minimum number of points. Pay special attention to these requirements.

Evaluation criteria often use descriptive words such as "should", "may" or "demonstrated". They may also use, though less frequently and in a different context, "optional" or "preferable".

Proposal Preparation: The Time Elements

The clock starts ticking from the time the RFP is issued. It is critical to plan your response time.

One of the key factors to discuss at the initial meeting is the need to create a realistic timeline for the proposal preparation. Monitoring this timeline will ensure that you immediately highlight problem areas such as people not completing their sections on time. Of course, in any timeline you allow for contingencies – in other words you allow for something to go wrong. When creating this timeline, allow time for the final production, inspection and delivery of the final product. It is highly recommended that, regardless of the structure requested by the RFP, you allow for your proposal to be modular. In that way, correcting one section does not require reprinting the complete proposal.

Regardless of the size of your firm, an initial meeting will need to be held. In small firms this may be only two people – you (who are to prepare the bid) and your boss (who conveys this fact to

Writing the Proposal

you). In larger firms, there are more people involved and the process becomes more complicated.

This kick-off meeting should not take place until the RFP has been read. There are often important points that need to be discussed.

The timeline evolves along the following line:
1. Decide who will attend the initial or "kick-off" meeting
2. Initial or Kick-off meeting
3. Section planning, research and development – mandatory and rated criteria
4. Contracting with sub-contractors if needed
5. Section writing
6. Submission of Sections to Proposal Manager
7. Proposal Manager refers Section to Red Team
8. Red Team Reviews, returns to Proposal Manager
9. Proposal Manager to Section Leaders
10. Rewrites
11. Repeat 5 through 9 as needed
12. Consolidation of Proposal
13. Verification of Consolidated Proposal
14. Production of Final Proposal
15. Verification of Final Proposal
16. Delivery of Final Proposal

There is more to this than just the above. Often Section Leaders will talk with each other to avoid duplication. In addition, there is still the need to ask questions of the customer during the process.

Final Review

This is critical. Review is a Red Team responsibility. However, the final review is both a Red Team and Proposal Team responsibility. Many proposals have been lost due to a lack of time for this final review. Allow as much time as you can spare for a page-by-page review, checking all computations and cross-referenced. Also, re-verify "mandatory" requirements. As already stated, your proposal should be modular.

More than one proposal in response to a RFP has had a section duplicated by error. The unfortunate fact in these cases is that no one checked the proposal to ensure that all material was properly placed. A section duplicated often means another section was omitted. The missing section may have been critical. The result may be that a bid is lost which should have been won.

The final review is to ensure that all elements are there, the certifications are present and signed, the pricing is complete, computations are correct, and decimal points are correct, the proposal is properly formatted and organized and that the proposal is signed.

It is vital that time is available to do a final proofread. Simple language errors will cause major problems. "We are not going to do....", is completely different from, "We are now going to do..." The only difference in the statement is a "t" instead of a "w". A simple typing error such as this could cause your proposal to be unsuccessful. This simple error would NOT be found by spellchecking the document.

Amendments to RFPs

It is not unusual for a complex RFP to raise many questions requiring many answers. This can result in changes, often significant, to the RFP. As a result, an amendment to the RFP may be issued advising of an extension to the closing date.

Another possibility is that due to complexity or sensitivity, you may have unavoidable delays in gathering information or preparation. If you know that this is the case, do not hesitate to request a time extension to the RFP. This is considered a win/no lose situation. The worse case scenario is that you receive a "no" to your request. This would leave you exactly where you were before you made the request. The best case scenario is that you receive a time extension.

How to Respond to a RFP
Winning Proposal Writing

4. The Red Team

Red Team Review

You may call it a review team, a validation exercise or whatever else you want to. The most common term used is the "Red Team". This is the team that does formal reviews of the RFP and subsequent amendments. It also reviews draft proposals and revisions to ensure that a high quality compliant proposal is submitted in response to the RFP.

It is important to understand who should be on the Red Team and the role of each Red Team member. Failure to clearly understand these elements leads to the mistaken belief that the Red Team concept fails. Red Teams, properly run, dramatically increase the odds of your bid being a winner.

As soon as the RFP is obtained by the firm and the Bid/No-Bid analysis is completed (perhaps even while this is being done), Red Team members should be provided with copies of the RFP. In fact, firms often have Red Teams already established and they participate in the Bid/No-Bid analysis.

The quicker the Red Team begins their analysis of the RFP, the better they can alert the Proposal Team as to pitfalls, contradictions, areas that need clarifying, etc. This saves valuable time and the cost of other resources by avoiding unnecessary work.

The role of the Red Team should be also be highlighted at the Kick-Off meeting as this is the team that will be doing quality control. The Red Team reviews are formal proposal reviews for accuracy, completeness and clarity.

Depending on the RFP, the Red Team role will emphasize different roles such as:
1. Evaluation of the RFP including recommending questions to be asked and monitoring RFP amendments and responses to the questions.
2. Evaluation of the proposal according to the evaluation criteria.
3. Consistency of message and soundness of strategy.
4. Completeness of message and demonstration of compliance.
5. Proof Reading.
6. Verification that all mandatory requirements are met.
7. Recommending improvements - The Red Team when they identify a problem will recommend a solution, suggest a rewrite, or recommend necessary technical input be obtained and inserted.

Composition of Red Team

The Red Team should be composed of experienced reviewers.

In particular, the manager of the Red Team should be an expert in the proposal review function, how the proposal should be prepared, and have an in-depth understanding of the RFP process and the RFP document. The Red Team Leader will ensure that full dialogue takes place between Red Team members and that the information and recommendations being sent to the Proposal Team are not disorganized or conflicting.

The people who are assigned to the Red Team must be independent from the proposal writing function. This means that senior management cannot be involved with the Red Team. Management will have input into the proposal writing, not into the proposal review. To do both functions creates a conflict of interest situation. Management participation will bias reviewers. When management is involved with the Red Team, the objectivity of the Red Team is impaired. Red Team members may not want to contradict or criticize management's input.

Therefore, to ensure a fair evaluation by the Red Team of the proposal, management should not be involved.

For most requirements, Red Teams are small and limited to one to three members. Although they may be a combination of outside professionals, specialists, and employees, they are normally one or the other. Outsiders have the advantage of bringing objectivity.

Responding to the Red Team Review

When the Red Team comments are received, an action plan needs to be in place on how to handle them. This can be either informal or formal depending on the complexity of the RFP.

There is no issue of who owns the draft proposal. The Red Team will provide a separate written report on the draft but never edit the draft directly. In this way, control of the draft remains with the originator. When the Red Team comments are received, the originator has one of two decisions to make – ignore the comment or edit the proposal.

Red Team Failure

When Red Team failure takes place, it causes people to criticize the Red Team concept. However, the failure is not with the concept; the failure is with the implementation. Some of the common reasons for the failure are listed below.

1. Red Team members only comment on errors/omissions.

Fairly may be due to improper instructions. Red Teams are created to help improve the proposal. In other words, Red Teams are there to assist in creating a winning proposal. This means that they suggest solutions to problems, offer helpful suggestions, suggest improved wording, do gap analysis (missing information). Red Teams will recommend rewording a document for improved clarity, suggest questions that should be asked and spot contradictions. The list goes on but it is important to recognize that the Red Team is not a role limited to only spotting errors. Although the Red Team does not have authority to rewrite the proposal, the Red Team observation may contain a suggested rewrite.

2. The Red Team is formed too late.

Contrary to some beliefs, you can never form your Red Team too early. Many firms have the role pre-assigned and ready for any forthcoming RFP. There is a fallacy that reviewing an incomplete document is a mistake. Large proposals are written by different authors and the sections developed at different times. As each draft is ready, it should be submitted to the Red Team. Errors between versions often occur and the Red team will be able to spot these. As well, there may be amendments to the RFP. The Red Team will be aware of these and will watch for how the amendments will affect the writing (or rewriting) of the various sections. The Red Team never directly edits a version. The versions submitted remain intact. This is helpful as the Red Team is able to look for suggested changes and improvements between versions. In this way, oversights will be more readily spotted.

3. Lack of Knowledge by Red Team members

This is a serious failure. Performing the Red Team role requires training. A person has to know what to look for, how the parts fit together and how the end product should appear. Red Team members are normally middle management or experts who know how the parts fit together. The solution is to have a Red Team consisting of experienced and inexperienced people. However, your experienced member must be dedicated to the Red Team review only. Guided by the experienced members, the inexperienced members gradually gain knowledge and become experienced.

You should never, on a complex procurement, have an inexperienced Red Team. If you are faced with this dilemma, you should hire an outside firm who can perform the function. In fact, on complex RFPs, it is always a good idea to consider hiring outside experts.

4. Red Team is disorganized.

This is caused by a leadership void. The people who are writing the proposal are accountable for their work. The Red Team is accountable for their work as well. Even if there are only two people on the Red Team, there has to be someone in charge. That person organizes the work, sets the tasks, decides how the reviews are to be handled, coordinates the reviews received from the authors, and returns it to them with the comments.

Error Avoidance

Firms have tried to avoid problems with the Red Team concept by creating other sub-teams of the Red Team, which are usually called by a different colour (pink, blue, gold, etc). While it is important to be organized, this does not solve the problem. The Red Team when properly constructed, works. Sub-teams (whatever you call them) increase the difficulty of coordination, make integration of the proposal more difficult, and can cause conflict.

One item the Red Team should avoid is the financial bid. The only responsibility of the Red Team is to ensure that the financial proposal is in conformance with the RFP. The Red Team, if it has knowledge of previous pricing, should offer comments on the structure and pricing used.

However, as stated, the Red Team has no authority to change the actual bid prices. In many cases, due to confidentiality, the Red Team never sees the bid prices. There is nothing wrong with this. The firm may have a review of its bid prices done by experts in costing but this is a separate function from the Red Team.

In summary, the key is to stick with the definition of the Red Team and not to try and modify it. The Red Team is a quality control, improvement function for the proposal. The Red Team has no authority to change the proposal. It can only recommend changes. The Proposal Manager is responsible for the final decisions on the proposal content and is not a member of the Red Team.

When Not to Use a Red Team

There is a time when a Red Team approach will not work and it is necessary to recognize this. If the time frame is extremely tight, you might have to settle for a quick review or have the proposal team do a final review. The worst situation is a self-review. Correcting your own work under extreme time pressures is a recipe for a disaster.

The other time a Red Team may not be used is for the final assembly of the RFP including graphics, layout and printing. There may be no time left for a final check. This is a risk to avoid if at all possible.

On one proposal that I worked on as a Red Team member, there were extensive back and forth versions of different sections. Version control was carefully and correctly done. The assembly of the final proposal started early in the morning (approximately 9:00 am) with a 2:00 pm submission deadline. There was no time for the Red Team to review the final document. As it turned out, instead of placing the correct information in its spot, the assembly team inadvertently duplicated one section of the proposal. While this was inserted in the correct place in the proposal, it was also inserted in the spot where other information should have been placed. The correct information was thereby omitted from the final proposal. As a result, the firm lost a multi-million dollar bid since the missing information was critical.

Templates

Often a Red Team may produce templates (or guides) in relation to some evaluation criteria. This is to help the Proposal Team produce better responses to the criteria and improve the subsequent proposal.

A sample template has been produced as Appendix D. This sample is in response to the evaluation criteria that are in the Sample Complex RFP produced in Appendix C.

How to Respond to a RFP
Winning Proposal Writing

5. Managing Bad RFPs

There are problems in responding to most larger and/or complex RFPs. This comes from a variety of sources – different writers, complexity causing conflict, incomplete information, outdated information, etc.

It is informative to look at a few of the problems:

Micromanagement:
Instead of stating that they want a solution to a problem, the technical writer for the RFP defines exactly how a service is to be performed, the process, the tools to use and the specification for each element. By not presenting the overall picture, it eliminates innovation or improvements that may have occurred in the marketplace.

Lack of Specifications:
This is the polar opposite of micromanagement. The client has not spent the time necessary, does not have the expertise to understand their situation or they just don't know how to write clearly. Either way, if you can't understand the RFP, you can't bid.

Multiple Writers:
As already mentioned elsewhere, large complex requirements usually have several authors writing different sections. Contradictions in terminology and specifications occur due to a lack of coordination between the writers, the knowledge of the writers, and the different skills sets of each writer. The end result may be a RFP that has serious problems. Unfortunately, rather than take the time to properly vet the RFP, the clients leave it to the potential bidders to find and question these errors.

How to Respond to a RFP
Winning Proposal Writing

Structure:
The RFP, having been written in sections, may be poorly structured. Elements that you need to start working appear in the middle of the RFP or at the end (or even throughout). Elements that you need to complete the work appear at the beginning or the RFP, in the middle or once again, throughout. You have to track and organize the elements into a structure that makes sense.

Evaluation Criteria:
Occasionally there is a disconnect between the evaluation criteria and the Statement of Work. This is another symptom and result of multiple authors. In this situation, the RFP evaluation does not reflect the requirements.

For example, the requirement may have originally required an accountant to verify an element of the work. Due to a rewrite, what is now needed is a person who is certified by the Project Management Institute. In other words, a PM rather than a CA. The result is that the evaluation criteria remained unchanged and still asks for CA credentials to be evaluated even though there is no longer a need for this.

The other item that often happens is contradictions in work schedules vs. RFP instructions and evaluation criteria. The result is that the evaluation scoring does not reflect the schedule that the requirement calls for.

Missing Information:
More often than not, missing information is easy to detect. In developing the RFP, sections and information were deleted or added by error but the numbering scheme remained unchanged. The gaps in the numbering scheme indicate missing information.

Managing Bad RFPs

It can easily be that the RFP does not include instructions for the formatting of the proposal. For example, the RFP states that the proposal is to be no more than 100 pages. What is not stated are the font, size of font, margins, size of page and spacing of lines. To ensure a fair and equal playing field for all firms, the information has to be the standard.

Similarly, gaps in the evaluation criteria also happen. It is incumbent on any bidder to total the marks in the evaluation criteria to ensure that there are no errors. You also need to know the relative weight, and try to understand the marks allocated to each section.

Solutions:
There are a few solutions available - guess, create alternatives or ask questions.

The best solution is to ask question after question. Any confusion works against you. If in doubt – ask. When you receive an answer and the answer doesn't make sense – ask another question. Your goal is to submit a high quality responsive proposal and you need the proper information to do so.

The next best solution is to create alternatives. This has to be carefully managed. Many RFPs expressly forbid this and insist that two (or more) separate proposals must be submitted. It is safer, but time consuming, to submit alternate proposals.

The worst solution is to guess. If you make an intelligent guess, you must explain it in detail and justify your assumption. This takes extra time without the offset benefit of knowing that your bid meets the requirements. Your bid may not conform to requirements nor be what is wanted your time may have been wasted.

How to Respond to a RFP
Winning Proposal Writing

6. Proposal Response – Elements

The more you respond to RFPs, the more you will observe similarities. They often request the same elements. However, there are also RFPs that contain minimal information regarding what and how to respond. In these cases, your experience will be of great use.

A meeting to discuss the different sections of the proposal should be helpful. First, it would help in understanding the various elements that are contained in the sections. Second, the discussion should help provide clarity in instances where the RFP is silent, poorly worded or vague. This clarity may be a better understanding of the evaluation criteria or a list of questions that need to be answered by the customer. Third, when you are submitting a proposal in a less structured environment with little guidance from the customer, the discussion serves as a guide to ensure that critical elements are not overlooked when you write the proposal.

Having this guide is also helpful when considering the development of the proposal. RFPs vary. You may or many not have a limit on the number of pages, have detailed evaluation criteria, have the format to respond dictated to you, or be allowed to ask questions.

A list of the various sections that will be discussed follows:
- Executive Summary
- Staffing Plan
- Resumes
- Corporate Experience/Past Performance
- Business References
- Technical Solution
- Management Plan
- Transition Plan
- Appendices

With RFPs, there are normally some evaluation sections that appear unique. However, although the titles change and the wording of the request is different, the sections that follow contain most of the elements that you will need to complete. For other evaluation criteria, many of the elements contained in the sections will be a useful guide.

Executive Summary

Overview:

Although RFPs differ both in what they are requesting and their evaluations, they tend to have similarities in the elements they request. Typically all responses to RFPs have an Executive Summary that briefly describes your company, what you are bidding on, how you will provide it, the benefits to the customer, and why you should be chosen.

The Executive Summary is the first item read and the start of the written communication with the customer. As such, it is an important part of your proposal. Although it is normally not a mandatory or rated requirement, the Executive Summary is essential as it sets the tone for the rest of your proposal. It has to be written with the focus on the customer. As such it should have a positive tone.

It should also be short, normally a maximum of only one or two pages, so that it does not conflict with or overwhelm the message that you convey in the rest of the proposal. Proposals that have a long Executive Summary lose the focus and the message that you want to convey. They may not even be read.

The Executive Summary makes clear that you are fully qualified to provide a highest quality service and look forward to working with the customer and states the benefits of doing business with your firm.

When To Write the Executive Summary:

There are three schools of thought on when the Executive Summary should be written.

The first is to write the Executive Summary immediately before you start work. This forces a firm (while they write the proposal) to focus on what they are going to say and how they are going to deliver the service. When you do this first, it helps the proposal team by providing a clear plan and rationale for your proposal. Your proposal will then be written to reflect this plan and rationale and to integrate the vision. It also allows you to ensure that all recommendations that follow can be accomplished by your firm. You are writing the Executive Summary from a vision, not from knowledge.

The second school of thought is to write the Executive Summary last. As you write a proposal, you learn what you can or cannot do as a company. You can address changes quicker without rethinking your approach. The Executive Summary that is written after the proposal is prepared will reflect what has been written in the proposal, not what you intend to write. Your Executive Summary will reflect a better understanding of the RFP, the evaluation criteria and your proposed solution. You are writing the Executive Summary from knowledge, not from a vision.

The third school, and most common, is a blending of the above two approaches. The first thing that is done is to create an Executive Summary. However, it is considered a draft, subject to change, revision or deletion depending on how the proposal develops. This helps give a focus or vision to the development of the RFP. This works well when you know that your proposal would overlook opportunities should you write the Executive

Summary first. You can change the Executive Summary as you write.

At the end, the Executive Summary is revised to account for innovations and changes. It is a helpful exercise to examine the difference between what was proposed and what was actually developed. With this method the probability of a poorer proposal being developed and causing critical time delays in writing, while various alternatives are explored, is reduced.

How Do You Decide?

The best approach for you is to determine what works for you as a team or a company and what suits your circumstances. Many firms are in a "focused" business already. In these cases, they leave the Executive Summary as the last item to be done. Other firms, usually larger, have many options that can be provided. Creating the Executive Summary first helps them coordinate the development of the proposal and eliminate less viable alternatives at the outset.

Executive Summary Checklist:

The Executive Summary Checklist should be customized to the needs and requirements of your firm. All the elements listed on the following page may not be required in your case. On the other hand, there may be elements that should be added. The elements are presented in no particular order. The order of presentation will be determined by your own requirements.

Proposal Response - Elements

Executive Summary Checklist

Item	Yes/No
Introduction	
Overview of our company from the evaluator's viewpoint	
Did we address the needs of the customer?	
Did we address the strategic goals of the customer?	
Did we address the challenges of the customer?	
Did we show that we are working for the customer?	
Our corporate culture and values	
Our firms reputation	
Testimonials	
Awards/Certifications	
Synopsis of what is being bid on	
How we will provide the service (solution)	
Why choose our firm (why us?)	
Benefits of our proposal (long term/short term)	
Key qualifications possessed by our firm	
Advantages of our approach versus the approach of competitors (ie. why we are best solution)	
Innovations	
"Fit" with customer's evaluation criteria	
Understanding of customer's perspective	
Importance of this project to our firm	
Key contact and contact information	
Did we keep language simple?	
Did we avoid use of jargon?	
Is the Executive Summary signed by th appropriate officer?	

Staffing Plan

Large complex procurements often have evaluation criteria that require information on how a project or service will be staffed. This means that the bidder has to prepare an organization chart, describe the duties of the people, how they will be staffed, and how they will be replaced if necessary.

The Project Manager

The Project Manager is a key position and who occupies it is equally important for both the customer and the bidder.

From the customer's viewpoint, the Project Manager is the key contact and the person who will be working closest with them. This is the individual that is expected to have authority to solve contractual problems as they develop. Therefore, the experience and credentials of the Project Manager will be examined very closely. In fact, it is normal practice to have this individual's qualifications as part of the rated evaluation criteria.

From the bidder's perspective, the Project Manager has the responsibility to ensure that the proposal is successful, to answer customer's queries and solve their problems. The Project Manager must know and understand the proposal. The responsibility for not letting the customer dictate new demands vests with the Project Manager.

Never indicate to the customer that you don't have a Project Manager or that the preferred Project Manager is working on other projects. If you don't have a qualified Project Manager, don't bid. However, there is nothing wrong with stating that the intended Project Manager is working on another project but, should you win, this individual will be reassigned immediately to the contract. Customers do not expect you to keep employees idle or under-employed while awaiting the award of a contract.

It is also common practice to request detailed information on other key people who will be involved in the link between the contractor and the client, as well as the individual with overall responsibility for ensuring the project or service is successfully accomplished.

Resumes for key people are normally requested. This will be discussed further in the next section.

Staffing Plan Checklist

The Staffing Plan should be customized to the needs and requirements of the proposal. A Staffing Plan template is presented on the next page. The elements listed may not be required and you may know of other elements to add. The elements are presented in no particular order. The order of presentation will be determined by your own requirements.

How to Respond to a RFP
Winning Proposal Writing

Staffing Plan Checklist

Item	Yes/No
Did we provide an organization chart?	
Did we provide a list of key positions?	
Did we detail the duties of the key positions?	
Did we explain how the positions will be staffed? ie. Existing personnel or new hires?	
Did we explain how we provide for replacement of personnel?	
Did we explain how we train replacement personnel?	
Did we explain how back-up is provided to allow for vacations or illness, etc of existing personnel?	
Did we name the key personnel?	
Were resumes of key personnel provided?	
Did we explain why our staffing plan/staff is better than the staff of another company?	
Do we need to explain/indicate how staff is supervised?	
Do we have low or high turnover? Do we need to explain why this is?	
Are we responsible for hiring client's staff who would otherwise be out of work?	
Is it expected that we will hire the existing contractor's staff (if there is one)?	
Did we address the level of effort (amount of work to be done) required by each person?	

Resumes

A RFP will often request resumes to be submitted with the Staffing Plan. Resumes are submitted to validate your firm's credentials and to show that you have personnel capable of doing the work and that they are fully qualified. When submitting multiple resumes, you should have a uniform appearance and format. There will be minor differences to highlight different areas of expertise for each person, but the overall appearance will be the same. This includes the same presentation order throughout all resumes – previous work experience, education, volunteer experience, etc.

It is helpful to keep in mind that this is a critical area where you are selling your people to the customer. Whether evaluated or not, many clients read the background experiences in a resume. Resumes must cover all the evaluation criteria but you should not limit yourself to only to the information necessary to meet the evaluation criteria.

It is also important to note that we are discussing professional resumes, not personal resumes. A personal resume will normally include an objective "why you want a job", personal references, etc. A professional resume may contain an overview and professional references regarding previous work.

Resumes are normally submitted as an Appendix to the main requirement. Although it appears to be a simple requirement, resumes are often the cause of major errors in proposal writing. Resumes are often outdated and submitted without tailoring them to the customer's requirements. It is common practice, but a mistake, to use "boilerplates" – resumes that are prepared for all uses and submitted - without tailoring them to a customer's requirements.

On the other hand, there are firms that try to customize every resume to match every proposal or customer need. This leads to a major difficulty in resume control. It can easily become a major difficulty to determine which version is valid and which version covers of which customer service.

The key question is "who is responsible for the resumes"? Is it the technical writer, a person from human resources, the person being proposed or a combination of these? The best solution is to have the person being proposed responsible for the content and accuracy of the overview resume. The technical writer or person from human resources is then responsible for the content and presentation of the information being requested. They accomplish this by interviewing the person being proposed.

Problems may stem from the need to ensure that the resume meets the evaluation criteria of the RFP. When the proposal is being assessed and an evaluator compares the necessary qualification to the evaluation criteria, they might discover that the resume does not match what is wanted. As a result the proposal may fail even though the person actually has the experience.

The best solution to this situation is twofold.

First, a resume control system should be instituted. A standard resume format for all personnel will help with this. Standard resumes are designed to be general, good for obtaining most jobs, but not specific to a client's needs. They should be kept up to date and adjusted at least every six months to reflect new learning and experience. A company can, without realizing it, end up with many different versions as they customize the resume to each requirement. Creating a standard resume format helps to standardize the process both of producing and evaluating the resumes

Second, the standard format resume can be used as written (boilerplate). The Red Team reviews the resume and advises what information is missing or unclear. Instead of rewriting the resume, a covering addendum is prepared and attached to the resume. This addendum amplifies and explains the qualifications needed for the specific RFP that is being answered. In other words, the addendum provides the information specific to each client's needs. To do this, you compare each resume with the requirements of the RFP to find out what is missing. You then work with the personnel whose resumes are being submitted to create an addendum that fills those missing gaps. The addendum is often quickly and easily created by the technical writer discussing the requirement with the proposed resource, and then writing out the missing information.

You may be given guidance by means of a job description for the position in question, or you may have to infer what the requirements are. In either case, the goal is to edit the resume or format the addendum in a way that is responsive to the RFP requirements.

Be specific. Make the relationship between experience and knowledge, and the proposal criteria very clear. Proposal evaluators will focus on the addendum to give them the critical information that they need. The end result is a resume that fits the evaluation criteria of the RFP. With this method, you track the addendum comments. The basic resume doesn't change for every requirement.

If resumes are not required, it is still a good idea to provide a summary of the backgrounds of the key team members that will provide the service. This is not a resume but rather a brief overview of each team member's experience and, most importantly, qualifications.

Resume Checklist

Resumes are documents that highlight your company's major assets – people. The resumes should be prepared to address the needs of your company. The elements listed below are presented in no particular order and may not be all-inclusive. A resume does not have to be chronological or cover all aspects of a career. Rather, it can highlight relevant significant and recent experiences.

Resume Checklist
(for each resume)

Item	Yes/No
Name, Contact Information	
Previous Work Experience	
Background	
Education	
Training and Qualifications	
Security Status	
Professional Credentials/Affiliations	
Volunteer Activities	
Awards Received	
Customized addendum provided	
Is the resume standardized (format, appearance, etc.)	
Does the resume address evaluation criteria fully?	
Contact information if applicable	

Corporate Experience/Past Performance

This shows the core abilities and skill set of a company. Normally this is written in very general language and is not well-tailored to a specific RFP. Even if the project work references are kept up to date, usually it is written as an overview and a summary of the projects.

As with resumes, it is recommended that a corporate experience and past performance control system be instituted. A standard format for all projects would be helpful to ensure completeness of information. This should be updated as new projects develop and are completed.

Proposal Response - Elements

Unlike resumes, the corporate experience needs to be adapted to each RFP if you wish to maximize the odds of submitting a winning proposal. You cannot use an addendum. Clearly demonstrate (relating it to the RFP requirements) your capability to do or to provide what you are proposing. You do this through detailed descriptions of your previous experience of tasks and requirements that were similar, and how you achieved them.

Corporate Experience (or Past Performance) often decides who wins the contract. It is the old adage that when hiring a dishwasher, you find "experience required" as one of the criteria. If you have never been a dishwasher, you have no experience. The circular rationale is complete with the question, "How do you get experience?" Evaluators and clients prefer to deal with firms that have a proven track record and this is demonstrated through Corporate Experience or Past Performance. It is generally assumed that the better the experience, the lower the risk is for the customer.

Professional References are often asked as part of Corporate Experience. These references are discussed in the next section.

Private Industry regards previous knowledge and experience as important – even more than the public sector. Private industry may use up to 40% of the total evaluation score based on previous knowledge and experience by the firm. This contrasts with the public sector which would normally have this as a maximum of 15% of the total evaluation score.

It is our experience that the number of companies that maintain an up-to-date past performance archive is small but that having this archive offers a competitive advantage. The usual case is that the past performance citations are out of date, incomplete, or non-existent.

How to Respond to a RFP
Winning Proposal Writing

Corporate Experience Checklist:

The Corporate Experience Checklist should be customized to the needs and requirements of your firm. Delete or add elements to meet your needs. It is suggested that the references be followed up with each client to ensure that they will recommend your firm. The elements are presented in no particular order. The order of presentation will be determined by your own requirements.

Corporate Experience Checklist

Item	Yes/No
Are the Corporate Experiences up-to-date?	
Do the experiences fit the time parameters (if any) specified in the RFP? Eg. Recent previous experience.	
Have you checked that all elements specified for corporate experience have been addressed?	
Have the number of projects requested in the RFP been provided?	
Did each of the projects address the technical expertise required?	
Does the Corporate Experiences have references and/or testimonials attached?	
Is all relevant Corporate Experience listed? This may/may no be requested in the RFP.	
Has sufficient in-depth detail been provided?	
Are you able to use subcontractors' experience to strengthen past performance?	
Did you address the time elements of the Projects? ie. Miestones - start date and completion date	
Was each Project/Past Performance edited to address the specific needs of the RFP?	
Are the Projects listed comparable in size to the RFP requirement?	
Did the Projects listed require comparable experience and expertise to the RFP requirement?	

Business References

References (when requested) usually relate to corporate experience and your ability to do the work. You will be asked to supply a list of projects that are similar in size, scope or contain the same work elements as the bid at hand. It is common to ask for client names, short profiles, and a brief case history.

You normally are requested to submit names that may be phoned, e-mailed or sent a letter, or you may be asked to submit a written letter from your references. In either case, immediately contact your "preferred" clients (the ones that you know will give a good reference). It is important to ensure that their contact information is up-to-date. At the same time, politely ask them if they will give you a reference.

In the case of written references, there is nothing wrong with writing the reference for each of them and asking them to print it under their letterhead and sign it. This is the best way to proceed if you want the references done in a timely fashion. People procrastinate and, if you don't write it for them, one or two will delay until it is too late.

Also, consider seeking more references than requested. This may save the day if one is delayed.

Business Reference Checklist:

The Business Reference Checklist should be standardized. It is used to verify all your reference information is complete. While it reflects the needs of your firm, the elements are generally the same for all firms. There should be a separate checklist for each project.

Business Reference Checklist

Item	Yes/No
Name of Project?	
Name of Client?	
Client Contact Phone Number included? (including cell phone)	
Client Contact E-mail Included?	
Letter from Client on file recommending your firm?	
Was Client contacted to advise that they are being used as a reference?	
Is Client information up-to-date?	
Is Client available to give a reference?	
Are you able to highlight the experience of your personnel through the references?	
Are you able to highlight the experience of your firm through the references?	
Will the client speak highly of your firm?	

Technical Solution

The technical section may be the most important part of the proposal and will be read carefully by the evaluators. It answers key questions in the evaluation criteria. Your response should outline your solutions to each requirement in the RFP. Creative solutions are encouraged as long as the solution is exactly what the customer states they need.

A Technical Section is not required in all RFPs. However, when asked for it normally becomes the longest section in the proposal. A technical solution will almost certainly have a high degree of commonality between potential bidders. This means that oversights and minor errors will become obvious. This reason alone makes it extremely important to provide clear, complete and well thought-out solutions.

When answering, use details to show that you understand the requirement, know of the challenges and have a methodology for solving problems. It is important to itemize your approach to doing the work.

Other elements are included in the technical section, such as the schedule for delivery or providing the service, and the contingency plan to ensure the service is successfully provided on time.

Also, there should be a list of equipment that is needed to provide the service. This includes such items as computers and software.

Technical Solution Checklist:

The Technical Solution Checklist will be highly customized to the needs and requirements of your firm. The elements listed on the following page are examples of what to consider and provide general guidelines.

How to Respond to a RFP
Winning Proposal Writing

Technical Solution Checklist

Item	Yes/No
Do we understand the client's present situation?	
Do we understand the need for the requirement?	
Were the technical requirements clearly explained?	
Were the objectives of the requirement clearly explained?	
Are we recommending a proven methodology to solve the situation?	
Do we have to develop new products/services to address the technical situation?	
Did we describe the technical solution in detail?	
Did we provide diagrams (if needed) to help explain the situation?	
Did we provide a flow chart for the solution?	
Did we explain the benefits of our technical solution?	
Did we provide a work plan for implementation?	
Did we explain/address existing or potential problems that need to be solved?	
Did we explain how we plan to solve these problems?	
Did we provide a schedule for implementation?	
Did we provide details on equipment, facilities or software that need to be provided for the solution?	
Do we know who provides equipment or specialized supplies? (ie. client or ourselves)	
Did we provide milestones for the implementation?	
Are some portions of the solution provided on-site and some off-site? Was this explained?	
Did we address/explain the need for specialized sub-contractors?	
Is there something unique about our solutions and did we explain this?	
Did we explain what tools and methodologies we use for all steps (eg. Design, workflow, tracking, etc.)	

Management Plan

This is the section that often differentiates one firm from another. A well-organized and clear thought process is essential. You need to explain to the customer how you will control and monitor the project or provide the service while at the same time you will allow the customer maximum input. Also, a reporting mechanism should be included to ensure that everyone knows the current status.

This section can also break down the roles and responsibilities of each member of the team, who they report to and how much authority they have to act independently. As part of this, you also need to explain how the work will be organized and how it will be supervised. A diagram of the team structure could be provided. At the same time, you explain how you relate to subcontractors (if any). Finally, don't forget to add who will be the point of contact for clarifications and the on-going work.

Before writing this section, re-read the RFP. Often the RFP will dictate what sections of the management plan need to be explained. Be careful to answer, in detail, each and every requirement that is specified in the RFP.

This is another area where pre-planning and, possibly, an outside consultant can help. It may be that your firm does not have good management plans prepared or have not written down the elements that focus on your different services and expertise. An outside consultant can help prepare generic management plans that highlight each of your specialties. In this way, you develop boilerplates.

The final product can be customized to RFP requirements. Although the elements will be constant, the actual management plan will be unique to your firm. This means that this is an opportunity to convince the evaluators why your firm is the best one for the job.

The result should be a clear, easy to read plan; one that your client sees as being sound and workable. Giving examples of how you successfully managed similar programs also helps your client to better and more favourably evaluate your proposal.

Management Plan Checklist:

The Management Plan must be customized to the needs and requirements of the RFP as well as your firm. It is essential to cover as many elements as possible. The elements listed on the following page may or may not be required in your case. The order of presentation will be determined by your own requirements. Although you may want to consider a course of action, you may not want to write about it. For example, you need to think about dispute resolution (what happens if something goes wrong between you and your client). On the other hand, you may wish to consider whether writing about it could imply that disputes often happen with your firm and create a negative impression.

Proposal Response - Elements

Management Plan Checklist

Item	Yes/No
Project monitoring	
Status Reports	
Quality Assurance	
How Organized (Team Structure)	
Organization Chart of the Team Structure	
Roles and responsibilities of key players	
Work place location	
Project Manager	
Key contact information provided (name, phone/cell, e-mail)	
Back-up provisions for personnel	
Major benefits that will result using this management organization	
Who manages the project/service	
Qualifications of management (expertise, experience)	
Why our management is better!	
Who is accountable?	
Dispute Resolution between firm and client	
Travel requirements	
Integration of Sub-contractors/Subcontractor plan	
Integration of Customer	
Scheduled meetings/milestones	
Project administration (scheduling, tracking, monitoring)	
Problem solving abilities (when things go wrong)	
"Working with" instead of "working for" the client	
Examples of previous successful (similar) management plans used	
Quality Control	
Risk Management	

Transition Plan

Many requirements do not require a Transition Plan as a new firm is being employed to provide a specific service with an end result. There is no on-going work associated with the requirement. However, there are often competitive RFPs that relate to on-going business requirements. Rather than negotiate forever with the same supplier, the choice is made to potentially transition to a new supplier.

The transition as described in the RFP will have specific points that have to be addressed. When a transition is requested, it may have far reaching consequences if not carefully written. A firm may agree to pay for some or be responsible for some of the transition costs or difficulties. The end result could be additional expenses and delays that could have been prevented or reduced. This statement holds true whether you are the new contractor with the transition from a previous contractor or the existing contractor who may incur costs with the transition to a new contractor. The time to protect yourself is when you are writing the proposal.

In discussing transitioning in, the incumbent contractor would appear to have an advantage. This may or may not be an illusion. The incumbent contractor, if doing the same work, has no transition. With updated technology, innovations and new approaches, the incumbent who scores better in the transition evaluation may score worse in other criteria. Repeating the past could easily become a liability not an asset.

The normal situation is a new requirement written in the RFP that means the incumbent contractor will have to transition. The way that they are presently doing the work will have to be changed to meet new demands by their customer. The other possibility is that the RFP addresses a new requirement which means no incumbent exists. All firms start with an equal playing field.

Proposal Response - Elements

If you are the incumbent, use this knowledge to your advantage. Explain how you know the requirement and, therefore, do not require a transition period. If the requirement has changed, you can explain how being the incumbent will make transition seamless as the improvements or changes are made. As incumbent, avoid the "Incumbent's Disadvantage". Don't take transition for granted. Be innovative if possible. Just as with a new contractor, document the step by step procedures governing phasing in new requirements.

If the transition is being evaluated, review how transition is scored. Ensure all concerns and points raised are addressed. If transition is not being evaluated, you should still prepare a Transition Plan. There is a cost to Transition and it will affect your financial response to the RFP.

Transition Plan Checklist

There should be two Transition Plan Checklists created. One for transitioning "in" when you gain the new contract, and one for transitioning "out" when the present contract expires. The concerns of each will be similar but different. The two Transition Plans will be customized to the services that your firm provides. The Checklist on the following page does not distinguish between the two Transition Plan checklists.

How to Respond to a RFP
Winning Proposal Writing

Transition Plan Checklist

Item	Yes/No
Transition Organization	
Employee Considerations (Recruitment/Layoffs, Workload)	
Key staff required	
Staff to be transferred form existing firm to your firm	
Implementation (In or Out) logistics	
Facilities (required or surplus)	
Transition Team structure/organization	
Involvement of incumbent or new contractor	
Scheduling	
Training required?	
Inventory/materials to be transferred	
Equipment to be transferred	
Software/records to be transferred	
Phase-in and/or phase-out	
Time elements involved	
Degree of customer participation/involvement	
Risk mitigation strategy	

Schedule

This is where you explain, if necessary, the timetable for the project. A flow diagram is an advantage, with milestones indicated and explained in a narrative. Part of the schedule is to explain future challenges and how you would overcome them.

Schedule Checklist:

The Schedule Checklist should be relatively standard for all firms and all requirements. Scheduling is a process and it is only necessary to ensure that nothing is missed in planning a schedule. The presentation below can still be customized. The order of presentation will be determined by your own requirements.

Schedule Checklist:

Item	Yes/No
Flow diagram	
Start and completion date identified	
Narrative attached	
Timetable/Timeline respected or explained	
Milestones indicated	
Tasks indicated	
Is the timeline for each task indicated?	
Contract Administration identified (meetings, etc)	
Gantt chart or other chart used	
Is schedule realistic?	
Does schedule match client goals	
Does schedule indicate problem with client goals?	
Is a transition period necessary (phase-in or phase-out)	

Appendices

In order to keep the length of your proposal to a manageable length, place material in appendixes. You do not want to obscure what you are offering. Using appendices effectively de-clutters your proposal.

Some items that should be in appendices are: the corporate description of your firm, resumes of key staff, and technical manuals or brochures supporting statements in your proposal.

Subjects often included in separate appendices are:
- Resumes of key employees. This has already been discussed as a separate section.
- Corporate brochures and assorted hand-out material
- Letters of Recommendation
- Lists of Projects/Previous Experience
- Corporate Profile/History
- Technical papers, blueprints, reports, etc.
- Newspaper articles, etc. regarding your firm's technical or service accomplishments.

Whether formally evaluated or not, firms often add supporting documents they believe will aid the customer in understanding their firm's expertise, knowledge and what makes their firm better than the other bidders.

7. Boilerplate

Wikipedia defines boilerplate as any text that is or can be reused in new contexts or applications without being changed much from the original. Boilerplates are an essential tool in large proposals.

Every proposal writer has access to and uses boilerplates. They keep in mind that boilerplates, properly used, save time in proposal writing. However they should be used with a caution. There are many variables from RFP to RFP, in the statement of work, the evaluation criteria and the terms and conditions. The time that they save in being used may limit the ability to show innovation and therefore cost points on the evaluation.

Resumes are an ideal place to have boilerplates. Properly prepared they do not have to be rewritten for every proposal and are subject to being updated periodically. The resume can be customized through an addendum to the resume.

Other areas that often have boilerplates already prepared are the corporate structure of an organization, the management plan, and previous projects successfully completed. Firms that are preparing proposals that are similar in nature are advised to create a library of boilerplates. As you receive feedback from bidding, your boilerplates become better and better. When needed, you can obtain a copy of a proposal that received a good rating and incorporate it into the proposal being prepared.

Although it is not considered to be such, technical specifications are types of boilerplates. A firm can resubmit them, unchanged, on numerous proposals. Boilerplates have to be edited to conform to the specific requirement.

How to Respond to a RFP
Winning Proposal Writing

When using a boilerplate it is helpful to have a few guidelines. First, compare the boilerplate that you are thinking of using to the requirement. Then tailor the boilerplate to the requirement. Remember, you are not only looking to add information to the boilerplate, you also have to delete information that doesn't fit. Review the requirement once more against the revised boilerplate. Is everything now addressed? Have you still included information that is not requested or is unnecessary?

Finally, keep in mind that every RFP will require different adjustments to boilerplates. Sections in the boilerplates may have to be rearranged. Even adjusted, a boilerplate will never fit completely the needs of the RFP evaluation criteria. However, it will be the best fit available. Boilerplate by its nature can add "padding" and therefore length to a proposal. Evaluators prefer to read shorter, to the point proposals. Boilerplates, by their nature, make trade-offs and may lack some focus

8. Graphics

The term graphics in proposal writing includes any visual supporting materials - artwork, flowcharts, graphs, etc. This area is one that the least attention is paid to but which is extremely important.

Although it should go without saying that graphics are visual and most people are visual learners. Therefore graphics, as a form of visual communication, is more effective than writing. Graphics are visual marketing and information tools.

Think about times when you have seen graphics used. Did they add to your understanding of the subject matter? If the answer is yes, then the writer was right to replace words with graphics. The easier the proposal is to understand, the more likely it will receive a favourable evaluation. It may be advantageous to use both narrative and graphics.

Deciding on a Graphic:

Until an RFP is issued and you begin to prepare your proposal, you don't know what type of graphic you need or want. As the proposal is being written, the Proposal Manager and the Proposal Team have to identify the graphic that they require.

It is not always easy to decide how to enhance your proposal or to identify the particular graphic that is wanted. This decision requires judgment and, while consistency must be maintained throughout all graphics, the decision to use a graphic can be done draft section by draft section. To simply their decision process, the Proposal Team could look to the use of bullet points for potential graphics. Graphics are often used to illustrate relationships, processes and trends. This book uses one example of a graphic. Each checklist of elements contained in various sections of this book is a graphic. Their presentation is consistent throughout the book. Each of these checklists illustrate a process, a list of steps, or thoughts.

The Proposal Team has to describe the graphic in detail to the Graphic Artist. Creating a graphic is not always an easy task and is done under time pressures. The Graphic Artist usually has to produce the graphic from scratch. Moreover, the graphic has to conform to the RFP instructions and the evaluation criteria, be visually appealing, and be produced on deadline. Even with computer assisted programming, this is a creative skill that has to be appreciated.

The Proposal Team has to consider the number, type and use of graphics. The type may include organizational structures, processes, reporting relationships, statistical trends, etc. Then they need to prepare a list of illustrations, charts, graphs, diagrams, etc. to give to the graphic artist. Too many graphics are just as bad as too few. But, no Proposal Team wants to overlook the opportunity where a graphic would enhance the proposal.

The Team also has to ensure that the information or data is valid. False information will cause the validity of the graphic to be questioned, and the validity of the complete proposal to be questioned.

Some of the decisions that the Proposal Team need to consider are listed below.

Graphics

Decision

Item	Yes/No
Does the graphic we want to use already exist?	
Do we have a sufficient number of graphics identified?	
Is there anything written that a graphic could enhance?	
Are any of the graphics prepared unnecessary?	

The following three sections (Needed, Clarity/Readability and Presentation) are to help ensure that each graphic will strengthen your proposal. Graphics deal with communicating a message to the client. This is of importance to the Proposal Team and the Graphic Artist to ensure that the evaluation of the proposal receives the maximum score.

Needed:

Using graphics enhances your proposal by improving the clarity of your proposal and conveying information. However, to be effective, they must be needed. You have to understand why you have created each graphic. In other words, the following questions have to be answered:
- Why was the graphic needed? – to highlight a technical detail, to easily explain a point, to further explain or emphasize an important point
- Who is the intended audience? – a technical expert, an evaluator, etc.
- What graphic means are you using to send the message? – graph, visual representation of a fact such as an upward trend, organization chart, etc.
- Does the graphic effectively convey important information to the client?

How to Respond to a RFP
Winning Proposal Writing

In the public sector, there is little emphasis on limiting the length of the proposal. Few RFPs are issued with this stipulation. This is not the case for private industry. When the proposal pages are limited, a graphic can convey important information in less space than a written narrative. The graphic then becomes even more important as an aid in winning contracts.

The following checklist gives some thoughts to consider when making a decision about having a graphic.

Needed

Item	Yes/No
Is there valid reason for having the graphic?	
Is the graphic needed?	
Will it convey important information to the client?	
Is it focused on the right audience?	
Will it be understood quickly?	
Is using it better than text?	
Does it enhance the text?	

Clarity/Readability:

Not only must a graphic be needed, to be effective it must also be readable and easy to understand.

The amount of space devoted to graphics depends on the proposal being submitted in response to an RFP. Some will have almost no graphics as the information requested is straightforward. Some, much more technical, may have over 50% of the proposal as graphics.

It is human nature to look at graphs, charts, diagrams and pictures and expect to understand them immediately. That is considered to be the purpose of a graphic. While the graphic needs to have a caption, it must present the information clearly without a caption. Very few evaluators will take much time trying to 'interpret' a graphic.

When a graphic becomes highly complex it is no longer understandable. Either scrap it, or as a preferred alternative, break it down into several smaller graphics. The old KISS (keep it simple stupid) principle applies to all graphics.

When presenting a graphic, it should also be considered that a non-expert must be able to view the graphic and understand the concept behind it. When preparing a proposal, it may be wise to have a person who does not understand the subject matter look at the graphic. The non-expert is an excellent benchmark for clarity.

You cannot be certain who is doing the evaluation. Often it is a person with limited or little knowledge of the technical subject matter. They have to be able to understand the graphic. If it is unintelligible to them, you have a problem.

The power of visual materials is well recognized. It is acknowledged in some circles that bad buying decisions have been made due to the persuasion of high quality graphics that accompany the written text. Read the RFP closely. A few RFPs limit the graphics to black and white only or state that no graphics can be used at all.

The following chart is produced as a guideline in analyzing the clarity of a graphic.

How to Respond to a RFP
Winning Proposal Writing

Clarity/Readability

Item	Yes/No
Is the graphic too complex?	
Can a non-expert understand the graphic?	
Can the graphic be understood quickly?	
Does the KISS principle apply?	
Is the information conveyed factual?	
Is the information conveyed clean and concise?	

Presentation:

The presentation of the graphic is critical. Based on this, the graphic may or may not be looked at by the client. Your goal, of course, is to have all evaluators look at the graphic closely. To have a graphic that is going to attract the client, your graphic must visually simplify complex data or information. The visual effect of a graphic also allows for highlighting the most important points.

There are several elements in the presentation of the graphic that must be considered. The descriptive text describes the graphic and what it is represents. There is also the title or caption which must make the purpose of the graphic clear. A graphic should simplify data and present it in a way that highlights the most important points.

Next, there is the position on the page. Positioning includes placing it appropriately in the proposal, located with what it is describing. Never have it split between two pages.
Although it is not always possible due to the type of graphic (chart, etc), it is preferable that the graphic is presented "portrait", not "landscape", to increase readability.

There is the appearance and complexity of the graphic. The simpler the better. A presentation that is too arbitrary or cluttered

Graphics

with too much information will not be read or given much attention, or well understood.

Finally, there is the colour used in the graphic. Many simple charts or graphs can be presented in black only. Comparisons work best with different colours. Be aware that the colours must be consistent in all your graphics.

Presentation

Item	Yes/No
Is the descriptive text clear?	
Is the title clear?	
Do the text and title match the graphic?	
Is the graphic positioned on the page with the text?	
Does the graphic appear to have clean lines and a pleasing look?	
Is there the correct amount of colour in the graphic?	

Does the graphic work?

This section is titled appropriately, "Does the graphic work?" In other words, does the client understand and accept the message conveyed in the graphic and respond favourably to it.

When you have created a graphic, you have to decide if it actually works in the proposal or if it clutters up the proposal unnecessarily. Sometimes the actual message sent by a graphic will contradict the information contained in the written proposal. To aid in deciding if a graphic works, the checklist on the following page can be used as a guideline.

If you check "No" for any category, this does not mean that you should not use the graphic. A "No" may be easily corrected with minor editing. Also, there are many reasons why you may want to continue. This decision is the same as all other decisions in the proposal writing process. Judgment has to be used.

Does the Graphic Work?

Item	Yes/No
The descriptive text is short and to the point	
The graphic is positioned correctly on the page	
The colours on the graphic are pleasing and consistent	
The graphic is not cluttered with too much information	
The graphic is clear to a non-technical evaluator	
The graphic is in accordance with the RFP requirements and explains necessary information that must be included	
The graphic enhances the RFP evaluation criteria	
The caption for the graphic matches the graphic content	
The graphic message can be understood without the captions	
The graphic presentation covers necessary information (years that need to be demonstrated, flow chart from beginning or project to end, organizational chart)	
The graphic adds to the explanation of the proposal and does not detract from it.	
Is the size of the graphic appropriate?	
The graphic addresses a client requirement that is needed even though it is not part of the RFP (innovation)	
The graphic enhances our overall bid strategy	
The graphic demonstrates our experience	
The graphic is easy to read.	

9. Version Control

Version control is vital. It is a risk control issue. In a large complex RFP, when you are writing and preparing your proposal in sections, there can easily be confusion. The contents of the sections can keep changing as new information becomes available. Your proposed solutions may change. The various authors can, and will, have different writing skills.

The worst case that I have witnessed in my buying career was over 250 questions being submitted on a RFP resulting in more than 250 answers. Many of the questions had been initiated as a result of earlier answers. The result was the information that had to be written in the proposal kept changing. In a situation such as this, it is critical to keep control of the changes in order to produce a solid proposal.

If you don't have a good control, as old versions replace newer versions, confusion can result. You must have a file naming convention that is simple and understood by everyone who is writing a section of the proposal. This will allow you to immediately identify newest versions and the older versions.

Version tracking will provide an audit trail that will be invaluable in developing the proposal. With the proper records, you can quickly see who made the changes. This allows you to promptly address problems or ask questions as to why the change was made.

The Proposal Team normally prepares sections of the proposal separately with the result that the Red Team analyzes these sections separately. Never delete your older versions of the sections. RFPs are nearly always amended. There are times that information will need to be retrieved from an older version due to a change in the RFP. If you have deleted the information, you will have to start over.

Just as the Red Team is not involved in writing the proposal, it should never edit a version. The Red Team is a quality control and review function. Although it may seem less productive, the Red Team must always submit a separate written narrative even if it is only to identify typing mistakes or punctuation. In this way, it remains clear that the Proposal is the responsibility of the Proposal Team.

It prevents confusion in version tracking since the Red Team does not edit/comment or revise versions. As an added but small responsibility, the Red Team will normally keep a record of versions to ensure that previous versions are not mistakenly given to it for analysis.

10. Empty assertions

Empty assertions are motherhood statements made without any proof of validity. It is fine to use them when writing advertising or promotional material. Used in a proposal, they damage the credibility of the proposer. They create doubts in an evaluator's mind since they are not substantiated. State only what you can prove.

Some of the statements are "we" statements. By that, it is meant that it is inwardly focused to the bidder – not focused on the client's needs. Others are meaningless, overused; they can be, and often are, used by most firms. Using them may be just a bad habit.

As a general rule, they should not be used in a proposal. The exception is you may choose to use a few of these words or phrases in the Executive Summary which briefly describes your company, what you are bidding on, how you will provide it, the benefits to the customer and why you should be chosen. It is the first item read and sets the tone for the proposal.

Some meaningless words or phrases are listed below.

Best Value:
This is meaningless. Best value in the client's viewpoint will be the resulting contract from the RFP process. Are you seriously telling them that there is no point in evaluation other bids?

Best of Breed/Best of Class:
Everyone states this. Don't just say it, prove it with examples of how your firm excels.

How to Respond to a RFP
Winning Proposal Writing

Comprehensive Solution:
This is an oxymoron. Do you ever offer solutions that are only partly comprehensive? In other words, solutions that partly work.

Customer first:
Very overused and not believable. It is advertising jargon. All firms consider that they put the customer first. In the RFP process, clients are looking for content, not advertising slogans.

Dedicated to:
There is no meaning to this statement. If you are bidding then it goes without saying that you are dedicated to fulfilling the client's requirement. Following the reasoning to its conclusion, it implies that you are not dedicated to other clients. The evaluators are looking for performance.

Excellent Customer Service:
Absolutely meaningless. Is there a firm that has prepared a proposal that offers mediocre customer service? Every firm could state this.

Fast Growing:
Are you supposed to say "slow growing" or "stagnate" if you are not "fast growing". This statement is in the context of your firm. The exception is when it is not about your firm. For example, you may refer to a fast growing industry.

Full Service:
One of the vaguest and most meaningless statements possible. Every one has a different interpretation. Using this term could cause serious trouble if you win the contract. Your definition of full service may not be the definition that the customer uses.

Great Reputation/Great Firm:
Define great. It has so many different meanings that it is meaningless.

Empty Assertions

Innovative:
Every firm considers themselves innovative. No firm will state that they do not welcome change.

Leading:
Leading company, leading edge, industry leader, etc.
While there may be a leading firm in an industry, all firms have specialties and lead in some respect. Are you going to write that you are a "following" firm?

Low Risk:
Another meaningless phrase. In proposing solutions that solve or address a client's need, is any firm going to propose a "high risk" solution.

Our highest priority:
This is an unbelievable statement unless you are stating, "Our highest priority is to win the bid." Priorities change.

Quality focused:
Unless you are answering a specific question on quality this is another form of meaningless motherhood statement. All firms will state that they are quality focused.

State-of-the-art technology:
One of the most overrated and overused expressions. Everything seems to be state of the art. No firm ever states that they use older technology that is proven and still effective.

State of the art:
Same comment as for state-of-the-art technology.

The right choice:
Every firm considers that they are the right firm for the job.

How to Respond to a RFP
Winning Proposal Writing

Top Firm/Top Quality:
Every firm will state that they are the top firm and produce top quality. No firm will ever state that they do mediocre work. This has to be proven.

Trustworthy:
Trust is earned not given. No one can consider a statement about trust as meaningless. However since it cannot be proven it is not valid.

Uniquely qualified/The only one:
Competitive bids by their nature mean that no one firm is "uniquely qualified". Statements to this effect damage the credibility of a proposal.

We believe/We think
In the context of a proposal, statements that have no commitment are meaningless. What you think or feel is immaterial.

We understand/We assume:
This statement demonstrates a lack of understanding regarding what the client wants. Never indicate to the client that you are not certain of their needs. How can you propose a solution if you lack information and have to make assumptions? Tell them how you will solve their problem in positive terms.

We intend to:
Intents have no validity in a proposal. They are not legally binding and cannot be evaluated, especially since your intentions may change.

We hope:
This is another meaningless statement. There is no commitment being made. In fact, this could be interpreted as a statement that

you are not certain that you can do anything, which is why you "hope".

Want your business/Desire your business
A valid statement but one that goes without saying. If you didn't want the business, you wouldn't be submitting a proposal.

We are committed:
You may be committed to fulfilling the contract, delivering on time, customer service or many other possibilities. It really doesn't matter. If successful, your proposal becomes a contract and you are legally committed. To state the obvious is not necessary.

We will try/we will attempt
This is a good-will statement and not a commitment. It can't be evaluated and you can't be held to it if you don't succeed. As with the "we hope" statement, it could be interpreted as a statement that you are not certain that you can do anything.

We can provide:
This statement is often a mistake and is meaningless in a proposal. Many times it is just a matter of how the proposal is written. Many writers will write, "We can provide" when the statement should be "We provide". "We can provide" is a statement that you are able to provide, not a commitment. "We provide" is a commitment.

We value:
This is another statement that is meaningless. It is a form of motherhood statement and not a statement of commitment.

World class/World-renowned:
There is no definition of world class or renowned. Most firms are not international and can not claim this. Evaluators and clients do not

believe this type of statement and the credibility of the firm will be affected.

11. Presentation of the Proposal

The presentation of the proposal is rarely assessed for marks when the customer does an evaluation. However, a firm that takes care in how they present their proposal, will be a firm that takes care how they do the work. In other words, a firm that pays attention to small details such as the presentation, is a firm that will pay attention to important small details in providing the service.

The format of a proposal is straightforward. First, it is recommended that when responding to a competitive RFP, you follow the instructions. Use the same format and numbering system as the evaluation criteria – whether or not you agree with that system.

So that the client always is aware of your company, ensure that your company's name appears on every page. It is preferable to put it in the header instead of the footer as there is a psychological advantage to being on "top" of everything. However, this decision is up to you.

Presentation is of some importance. Use new binders if you are using inserts, and have all pages correctly and professionally three hole punched. If using spiral binding ensure that there is a cover page protected by plastic. Ensure that there are tabs to separate key sections. In all cases, ensure that the content can be quickly identified by the cover.

Often there are no instructions as to the layout. In that case, other than ensuring all evaluation criteria is addressed, there is one solid principle to follow – readability. Ensure that you don't overcomplicate your language. It is important that your proposal can be read easily and effectively and that all information can be easily located through cross referencing.

How to Respond to a RFP
Winning Proposal Writing

It is recommended that the font be Times Roman or Arial, 10 or 12 point or equivalent. If you are using 8 ½ "x 11" paper then margins should be 1" on all four sides. For ease of readability, it is also recommended that the spacing between lines should be 1.5.

Graphs and charts should be clearly identified and labelled.

Finally, there should be a Table of Contents for the complete proposal.

12. Pricing Strategies

For most proposals, the financial proposal is separate from the quality evaluation. The goal is to maximize your point score on the quality evaluation. That will lessen the impact of pricing. The difference in the strategies is the changing emphasis on some of the elements of the proposal.

The structure of the financial proposal in a RFP is usually predetermined. You must follow the grid or template provided in submitting your bid – even when you know there are problems with the structure. In a recent bid, the RFP required the bidder to provide subcontractor prices for software to be in Canadian dollars. The problem was that the subcontracted supplier for this software was in the USA. This meant that the exchange rate had to be considered and, as recent experience has shown, it can fluctuate considerably. The bidder, in a written question, suggested that this portion of the financial proposal be in US dollars. The customer refused. The result was the proposal had a considerable mark-up as a risk mitigation strategy. The firm won the bid and unless the exchange rate becomes very unfavourable, will make more money from assuming this risk than from the rest of the contract.

There are just three pricing strategies available on any proposal.

1) You expect to bid a higher price than the competition

It is critical that your written proposal justifies the higher cost. This is a difficult situation as the rules state that evaluators will not see your financial proposal until they have completed the quality evaluation. However, within the written narrative, you can emphasis the features that have a higher cost. Emphasize the quality of your proposal.

How to Respond to a RFP
Winning Proposal Writing

Emphasize the reduced risk with your firm. Lower cost means lower quality of results. Low cost may also mean a longer time taken to accomplish the service due to a lack of committed resources. Lower cost can also interfere with continuity of service. Show how your bid avoids these risks.

Also, in your proposal, make the client aware that you are sensitive to cost and it is your productivity that will reduce the cost.

2) You expect to bid a lower price than the competition

This is less of a worry if the financial proposal and the rated quality evaluation are separate. You now want to position yourself with the client and defend against the higher price justifications (point 1). Use the same themes as in point 1. Demonstrate how there is reduced risk with your firm. Show that you are sensitive to cost and that is why you are priced lower. In your proposal, demonstrate that you are customer service oriented.

3) You don't know whether your bid will be higher or lower

This is the normal case in the majority of bids. Usually you know your main competitors and have an idea how they price themselves. The key is quality. Show how you add value to the proposal and work hard to maximize your scores on the rated evaluation.

13. Proprietary Information

Bids are meant to be confidential. The information that you provide is not to be used for the benefit of another bidder. In many proposals the information provided is somewhat generic. The general approach and methodology will be recommended by all bidders. However, your firm is unique and there will be unique elements in your solution that other firms may not have thought of.

Although you are bidding to win, there is the possibly that you will not be successful. In that case there is a danger that the methods you would use to provide the service, or meet the technical aspects of a good, will be used to help the successful firm. Your solution may be innovative and you do not want other firms to gain from your intellectual property.

A confidentiality statement (non-disclosure agreement) is the way to address this situation in every proposal. In other words you are stating that the information being provided is confidential. You also state that the information in the proposal can be used solely for the purpose of bid evaluation. This information is to be disclosed on a "need to know' basis for bid evaluators.

This notice is usually the first page in the proposal. It is often repeated at the beginning of every major section. The following example is used for illustration purposes only. It is recommended that this clause be written by a lawyer for your firm. As this clause will be used on every proposal, the legal cost becomes negligible.

How to Respond to a RFP
Winning Proposal Writing

Confidentiality:

This proposal contains information that is confidential and proprietary. Any use of the information contained herein is not permitted without the express permission of (name of company).

14. Think Like an Evaluator

Evaluation – an Evaluator's Perspective:

Evaluators are obligated to follow the evaluation criteria as written. It is therefore important to understand how to read evaluation criteria. Not all evaluators will analyze in depth but you have to write your proposal with the assumption that you are going to have the toughest most expert evaluation possible.

The ability to analyze the rated evaluation criteria is a Red Team function. This ability may also be the most important element in ensuring that a good proposal is produced.

When you are preparing your proposal, normally you don't know who will be doing the evaluation. It is a mistake to assume that evaluators are technical experts. Furthermore, it is also a mistake to assume that evaluators know how to evaluate.

Evaluators are people. They have different backgrounds, different evaluation skills and abilities, different technical knowledge (ranging from very little to expert) and different expertise. They also may come from different parts of the organization which affects their viewpoint – managers, technical personnel, users of the service, etc.

Even people who have evaluated proposals previously may not know how to evaluate properly. To add one further complication, even when they have the same expertise, they also have different points of view and different preferences as to proposed solutions.

Therefore, you cannot depend that the evaluators will be expert evaluators. Your proposal should be designed so that evaluators don't have to know anything. This makes writing in clear, understandable language even more important. It also means avoiding the use of jargon or trade references without explaining the meaning in detail. You should "Think like an evaluator, so that the evaluators don't have to think".

Evaluating:

A common problem with some RFPs is a disconnect between the Statement of Work which tells you what the client wants and the Evaluation Criteria which tells you how it will be evaluated. This can cause a problem for evaluators. They are limited to the "how it will be evaluated" even when they know there is an error. It is too late when an evaluation problem is found after the bids have closed. In these cases, they have to evaluate in the manner that was requested.

These errors are not always obvious. There was an RFP issued that had one of the rated evaluation criteria requesting reports with accounting information. There were eight bids received. During the evaluation it was discovered that every firm had different interpretations of what had been requested. Rereading the evaluation criteria (in hindsight) the customer's evaluators realized that it was obvious that any of the interpretations could be valid. The solution proposed and used by the evaluation team was to award all bidders full marks. In this way the evaluators did not penalize any firm for the error in the wording.

Evaluators follow a guide when reviewing your proposal. The exercise is methodical. First they verify any mandatory requirements and then move to the rated criteria. Their goal is to eliminate proposals, not to pass them. At the end of the process they will usually have just one proposal left. This proposal belongs to the firm who will receive the contract. To make their life easy, it is essential that you meet each and every RFP requirement.

Mandatory criteria are meant to be evaluated on a pass/fail basis. With regard to all mandatory criteria, I recommend that the proposal starts off with a statement such as, "We fully meet the mandatory criteria of ... as follows." In this way, you eliminate the evaluator being able to question the response, thinking, "I don't know...." The evaluator's options are limited to only two choices – to agree with your statement (yes), or disagree with your statement (no).

Don't use bafflegab when writing your proposal. Unnecessary, complicated information not requested in the RFP opens the door for interpretation and questions. Write straightforward statements.

On a relatively simple RFP, there were two proposals submitted. One was approximately 20 pages and the other 70 plus pages to answer the same rated evaluation criteria. The proposal of 20 pages received an evaluation mark close to 90%. The 70 plus pages received a bare pass, just over 70%. The evaluators' commented that the long proposal was confusing and it was hard to understand what was being offered.

Evaluation Process:

If there was only one evaluator, bias could easily set in. At a minimum, it would be easy for an unsuccessful bidder to accuse the client of bias. The evaluator could miss critical information in a proposal that would increase or decrease the scores resulting in a contract to the "wrong" firm. Therefore, there is always more than one evaluator. The number varies according to resources and need. The buyer is normally not an evaluator. However, the buyer is still accountable for the results being fair.

The evaluation process is relatively straightforward. Once all proposals have been received, a copy of each proposal is given to each evaluator. Instructions are given on how to evaluate. The evaluators normally work separately reading and assessing each of the proposals in any order that they choose. They write down their observations and the tentative score that they would give each proposal. None of this is considered to be final.

At this stage, subject matter experts may be consulted to evaluate only certain sections.

The second stage is to have a meeting of all the evaluators to discuss and compare observations. In this way the evaluators have the benefit of the observations of other evaluators. They may have read something that other evaluators overlooked or, overlooked something that other evaluators read. Each evaluator now has the opportunity to adjust their scores based on these additional observations.

There may be some clarifications that are needed. These questions will be sent to the firms for response. Once the responses are received, the final scores for each evaluator are determined.

There are different methods of arriving at the final total score for the firm. The method must be decided before the evaluators meet to avoid bias, as different methods could produce different results. The most common method used is to obtain a consensus (all evaluators agreeing on the mark). Another common method is to total all the various evaluators' scores for each category and divide by the number of evaluators to achieve an average.

15. Defensive Proposal

Firms write proposals with the goal of winning the bid. There is nothing wrong with this but you must also think defensively. The concept of a Defensive Proposal is considering your proposal from the viewpoint of an evaluator. The evaluator eliminates bids (proposals) to determine the winner. What you want is to be "the last man (or person?) standing". In other words, you want "not to lose" – you are trying to avoid elimination.

Reviewing a proposal from a defensive position, changes your perspective. The questions that you keep asking is, "Am I giving the customer exactly what they want?" It also helps you write a proposal that is clear and which meets all the evaluation criteria set out in the RFP. This will reveal weaknesses in your proposal.

When reviewing from a defensive viewpoint (as opposed to a winning viewpoint), you realize that you might be exaggerating and overemphasizing some facts. You may also be adding unnecessary elements to the proposal. Again, the viewpoint is one of not losing points (as opposed to gaining points). You can often realize that you would actually lose points by giving them things that they do not want and not concentrating sufficiently on what has been asked for. This is normally part of the Red Team function.

Ideally, you have defined the customer's requirements, and proposed a solution that meets their requirements. When you write the proposal you prove that you can do what you have said. In other words, you close the deal with words and provable facts and assure the customer that they will minimize their risk by going with you.

The following example illustrates a defensive proposal:

How to Respond to a RFP
Winning Proposal Writing

Put yourself in the mind of an evaluator who has 8 proposals to evaluate. Every firm when starts with a clean slate. Somehow, someway the evaluator has to come up with only one firm.

"Round 1" will be to verify the firms that meet the mandatory requirements as defined. The evaluator will not be looking for completeness but oversights or errors. In the case above, 2 firms are found to have made critical mistakes in the mandatory requirements and there are now 6 firms.

The evaluators now start "Round 2". If the evaluation is out of 100 points, every firm starts with 100 points. In the above case, the pass mark was set at 70 marks out of 100. The evaluator now starts reading and examining each proposal. When they find a deficiency or oversight, they reduce the score. This process is not choosing winners, it is actually eliminating losers.

The results are in and 3 firms received over the pass mark of 70. Out of the 3 firms (although you don't know it), your firm received a mark of 86 and the other were 77 and 75. Only you bid on making the evaluator's job as easy as possible. Only you wrote your proposal from the evaluator's point of view.

Do you win the bid with such a high score? The odds favour your firm. However, there are no guarantees. The financial bid is yet to be assessed.

16. Bidders' Conferences and/or Site Visits

Within a complex competitive bid, the RFP often states that potential bidders may attend a Bidders' Conference or Site Visit of the location where the work is to be done.

Bidders' Conferences are held in a meeting room and are formal. They are part of the RFP process when the customer wants to ensure that bidders fully understand all elements of the requirement - technical, operational, legal, duration, performance, etc. Financial or security requirements may also be discussed.

The Conference is usually run as a formal meeting with a head table consisting of the contracting officer and technical specialists. You are usually required to sign in. A record of the Conference is kept and distributed, often as an amendment or addendum to the RFP. All potential bidders are able to attend.

Attendance is often mandatory. In other words, if you don't attend, then you are not allowed to submit a proposal.

Even when attendance is optional, bidders should always go. From a competitive viewpoint, they give the bidder the opportunity to ask questions and to observe who may be the other bidders, and how many of them there are. This information may result in a competitive advantage when submitting the proposal. It may also give you important contacts that you can team with to jointly submit a proposal.

At the Conference, listen closely to the questions and answers. The minutes may not completely reflect the clarifications. There may be questions that you do not want to ask as it would reveal a weakness of your firm or give away a potential competitive advantage.

With a Site Visit bidders see exactly how much work is required to be done, the space available to work in and also increase their understanding of the requirement. Important elements that need to be clarified may be observed, such as available electrical outlets.

17. Oral Presentations

In complex service procurements, oral presentations are common. Their purpose is to assess the ability and knowledge of the personnel involved in doing the work. On a long-term contract, these people will be working closely with the client and it is important, from the outset, to know that there will not be problems.

However, due to the nature of the oral presentation and the need to be "fair", future working relationships cannot be objectively evaluated. Therefore, evaluation criteria will be established that is impartial and measurable.

Following the premise that the presentation is to be impartial, the oral presentation will be rigidly structured. The length, location and format will all be identified in advance. The panel members will be predetermined and, if possible, the same panel will be used for all presentations.

When an oral is required, you should consider it an opportunity to reinforce and add to your message. Only those firms with a good opportunity to gain the final contract will be asked to present. The evaluation of the oral will have a separate score that will be added to the evaluation of the written proposal. This total score, factored with the price evaluation will determine the ultimate contractor.

There are a number of critical factors surrounding the oral presentation and they are discussed in detail in the following sections.

Preparation

Once you have been notified that you will be giving an oral presentation, it is important to prepare. The first step is to quickly gather any information that you can.

Immediately assemble a meeting of the potential presentation team. The work "potential" is used advisedly. Once assembled, you have to determine who should speak on which subject, who will hand out the material, etc. There are normally limits to the number of participants that you can bring. If they have not advised you regarding this limit, ask the question. You also have to determine who is to prepare what piece of information – Power Points, graphics, audio,

The RFP may have already spelled out who should be the main presenter. Normally, this is the Project Manager for the contractor. In the event the main presenter is not identified, it is recommended that the person who will be the main contact with the client (normally the Project Manager) should take the lead. The main presenters are required to be knowledgeable regarding all aspects of the proposal. Other presenters are specialists and have to show how they link to the main presentation but do not have to know all aspects of the proposal.

If they did not advise you regarding equipment that you can use or that will be supplied, you have to ask for what you require. For example, what kind of equipment is provided – laptops, internet, overhead projectors, audio connections, etc. and where the electrical outlets are.

Timing

Timing is critical for the Oral Presentation. Usually you are given a fixed amount of time to present in and a list of subjects that must be covered or questions that must be answered. The Questions and Answer session that follows the Oral Presentation is usually not considered part of the timed session.

Timing breaks down into two elements – preparing for the presentation and the actual presentation.

The first step is to select a Coach to prepare for the presentation. This is an excellent task to assign to the Red Team. The Red Team is responsible for quality control and, being impartial, can help organize a high quality presentation.

The coach is not responsible for content, but is responsible for timing and ensuring that the presentation is done in a controlled manner. The worst thing that can happen is for a presentation to be disorganized and not to respect the time limits that have been set.

The coach will time each element, ensuring the total time is within acceptable limits. This means that individual presenters have to be focused and stay on topic. While each element can be timed separately, there must be a minimum of two, and possibly three rehearsals of the complete presentation. The tone of the presentation must be positive and the elements must smoothly integrate with each other.

During rehearsals, cell phones, blackberrys, etc. are to be turned off. There must be no distractions. You will hear complaints about the amount of work and the time needed. The answer is that oral presentation is used for high dollar value, long term contracts. To do less than your best is to risk losing the contract.

Having the Red Team coordinate ensures the neutrality needed to help key personnel improve. When they obtain help in presenting and positive feedback in developing their presentation, they will do better. The rehearsal will help those less experienced in speaking in front of audiences and they will be more certain of their material.

At the same time this is being done, the visual Power Point presentation will have to be brought in alignment with the oral content.

At the actual presentation, the Red Team will not be attending. It is still necessary to have a timekeeper – someone to watch the time and ensure that the presenters stay focused on the presentation. This can be anyone on the presentation team. The key is to have a signal that can be used to tell the individual presenter that his/her time is up and someone with authority who can, if necessary, stand up, interrupt the presenter and keep the presentation moving. They would make a statement to the evaluation panel such as, "You have given us a limited amount of time to present our proposal to you. It is important that we cover all elements so we will continue on to the next subject. Should you have any questions about this part of the presentation, we would welcome questions at the end of our complete presentation." Hopefully, this would not have to take place. However, you do not want to run out of time with elements left unaddressed.

Room/Layout

If possible, it is important to know where you are going to do the presentation. The facilities, size of room, seating arrangements for presenters and evaluators, and equipment and electric outlet availability are important to know. The more you know about the room, the more you can be prepared. If possible, make a detailed scale drawing of the room.

Oral Presentations

If details are not given, ask for the necessary information. Are you able to see the room in advance?

Some potential questions are listed below:
- Room layout – conference table, U-shape
- Size of room
- Shape of room – long and narrow, square, L-shape?
- Type of room – normal, theatre?
- Lighting
- Equipment supplied – laptop, overhead projector
- Telephone lines (if needed)
- Seating arrangements
- Electrical plug-ins, service?
- Can you bring spectators? Where do they sit?
- Where is the location?
- Can you have advance access to setup for the presentation?
- Internet connection (if needed)?
- If windows, can these be shaded?
- Lighting (can you lower lights, turn off, front/back lighting)
- Can the furniture be rearranged for your presentation (if necessary)

Presenters

The most important person on the team is the person who will lead the oral presentation. Most companies select the Project Manager for this role. In this way the client gets to know the person that will be in charge of their project. They also will be able to assess his/her technical knowledge and experience and communication abilities.

In choosing the Project Manager or lead presenter, keep in mind that technical knowledge is paramount. You can teach the presentation skills. Understandably, firms often believe that good presenting skills are the key in an oral presentation. There is no denying this is important. However the technical knowledge and experience took years to develop while the necessary presentation skills can be taught relatively quickly.

Most firms have spokespeople who are used to dealing with the public or with clients. They may not be used to, or at ease with speaking to an audience. In any case, the main presenter may feel that the success or failure of the oral presentation is completely on their shoulders.

These people need extra help. Not only is it necessary to do the rehearsals, it is necessary to listen to them and reassure them that their fears and concerns are valid and not abnormal. Most presenters, even the confident public speakers, feel the pressure to be successful.

Coach them. The more that they know what is expected of them, the better they will become. Let them know that they are to be positive at all times. They are not to criticize the competition. Better yet, they should not even do a comparison to or mention the competition.

Reinforce that they are clarifying, not replacing, the written submission. You are proud of the work done on your written proposal. It can stand on its own as you would not be at the oral presentation if it had not. Presenters are to stay on-track, focused on your proposal. This is a major aid to building confidence as they should have in-depth knowledge of it.

Before any rehearsal or the presentation, ensure that your presenters are rested. Fatigue impairs the ability to learn or focus. They will need all their energy to be up-beat and dynamic during the presentation. A tired person will find it almost impossible to maintain a positive attitude.

Remember, the presentation should be interesting, not dull. The evaluators want to know that they can work with you and that they look can forward to the opportunity.

Handouts

Handouts are the least of your worries when doing an Oral Presentation, but they have the ability to make a large impression. There are Oral Presentations where you are not allowed to give handouts. Fortunately, these are rare.

Plan what you are going to hand out to the evaluators. Some firms use a copy of their Power Point presentation as their handout. This has both pros and cons. On the one hand, it allows the evaluator to follow your presentation and make appropriate notes. On the other hand, you may not be able to impress on the audience the important information that you wanted to.

In any event, the handout content must be consistent with your written proposal. It must also be consistent with the presentation. As a courtesy to the evaluators present you should plan on handing out material in both English and in French (if the client works in a bilingual setting).

Finally, ensure that you have more copies than you need. Allow for one copy per evaluator, one copy for each participant and have extra copies in case more people are there than you expected would attend.

Body Language

Depending on the literature that you read, body language is between 50% and 80% of our communication. Decisions on people are made within the first minute and, once made, take considerable time to change. Therefore the body language of presenters is critical.

Body language can demonstrate a positive or negative attitude. In fact, it can convey the exact opposite of what is being said to the detriment of the presentation.

Fortunately, body language can be improved during the rehearsals if the presenter is ill at ease. Experienced presenters generally have a relaxed body language that conveys openness, friendliness and professionalism to their audience.

When presenting, relax. Take the time to set yourself up. Place your team where you want them to sit. Then place yourself. Don't start until you are ready. Stand facing the evaluators, look them in the eye and start. Be aware that your gestures are cultural. English use less than French or Italian. The amount that you use is unimportant. The key fact is to ensure that they match your style and your speech.

The first item of business is to introduce yourself and then your presentation team. Name each of them, their background and their role in the presentation. If you have an observer, introduce him/her as well. Evaluators will take note, perhaps subconsciously, that you regard everyone as important.

If you are relaxed, there is nothing wrong with moving around somewhat. Properly done, this can engage your audience. However, if you are moving because you are nervous, this will show.

The screen (if you are using one) should be used for talking points. When you want to make an important point, you should consider taking a step toward the audience. This way, through body language, you are able to emphasize the point.

Now that you have prepared, the missing element is, "Where are your hands?" This is a serious question. The following is a list of do's and don'ts for your hands.

"Do have open, not closed hands."
"Don't put your hands in your pocket."
"Don't fold your arms (shutting down); keep your body language open."
"Don't point at the evaluators; pointing for effect at your team or the slide is acceptable."
"Do keep your hands at your side or in front of you. Do not have them held behind your back."

Demonstrations

As part of the RFP process when purchasing commercial systems or services that require technology, it is common to request that demonstrations of the existing systems be done. In this way, the client avoids contracting with a supplier who can not do the work.

This is a form of "Show and Tell". It is your opportunity to demonstrate that your solution is superior to others. It also allows you, within a narrow scope that requires good judgment, to beta test innovations and enhancements that will be incorporated into your existing system. As such, it is another stage where rehearsals are important.

Depending on the RFP, this may be a pass/fail situation or evaluated in accordance with a predetermined marking scheme. In any event, this is still an oral demonstration. In this case, the main presenter should not be the demonstrator. The main presenter should stand when talking about the system. He/she will be assisted by the person who does the demonstration. This person is responsible for explaining the operation of the system to the client step by step.

At this point, the client (evaluators) may request to see specific operations. The demonstrator will be the spokesperson for this as they show the client the specific operation.

Doing the demonstration right is critical. Failure to demonstrate the system or failure to address a query due to lack of knowledge will result in your firm being eliminated from the competition. Therefore you must have an experienced, knowledgeable person doing the demonstration.

Questions and Answers (Qs & As)

After the presentation, there is a question and answer period. This is used to clarify statements heard during the presentation that were confusing or which may appear to conflict with the written proposal. This allows you to eliminate misconceptions regarding your services. To assist you and to avoid errors, bring a copy of the RFP and your response for all members of the presenting team. It is helpful to have both indexed with tabs so that you can refer to it and find the information quickly.

It also allows you to re-emphasize areas of your proposal that are your "strengths". Since you are giving an oral response, it is not hard to add messages. Plan these messages in advance. You can brainstorm and think of questions that may be asked. Answer them. By doing this, you can be prepare responses and messages. You are "anticipating the unexpected".

Although it is "pre-determined", set the stage. Tell the evaluators before you begin your presentation that you are looking forward to answering their questions. In the unlikely event that it is not part of the presentation, offer it anyway as a way to create a dialogue with the evaluators.

Oral Presentations

The main presenter does not have to answer all the questions. However, there must be an organized approach to this. The main presenter is the lead. He/she should direct questions to the appropriate expert. Follow-up questions to the same responder do not follow this protocol. They are answered directly by the responder.

Common courtesy is also important. When one person is answering a question, another should not simply jump in and add to the answer. Instead, they should indicate to the presenter that they would like to speak on this subject. The presenter is in charge and will decide when, or if, the individual can speak.

Be prepared to initiate the questions and answers. After completing the presentation, you may say words similar to, "That ends our formal presentation. We thank you for the opportunity to further explain our offering and look forward to answering questions. Does anyone have the first question?"

If no one speaks up, you can continue, "One question many people ask about our service is …? Of course you have already prepared your answer.

While some of the following tips are basic, they help with answering questions and serve as a reminder:
- Look at the person who is asking the question
- To avoid misunderstandings, repeat or rephrase the question before answering it.
- Ensure that the person who is responding to the question, makes eye contact with all the evaluators.
- Ensure that your body language remains relaxed.
- Don't shift around. Try and remain in one place so that evaluators do not have to focus on where you are rather than what you say.

- Answer completely without becoming overlong or wandering.
- Answer the question – don't critique it.
- Keep your answer short, concise and focused, not long and boring

Loaded Questions

It is worth considering loaded questions. Sooner or later, a presenter is going to be asked one. The best known example of a loaded question is, "Do you still beat your wife?" There is no good response to this. You cannot answer, "Yes." Equally, you cannot answer, "No." (ie. you no longer beat your wife).

The actual question may be more indirect (but still loaded). For example, "Why bother recommending something we don't need or want?" The advice to follow is to avoid answering a loaded question directly. It must be answered, but there are many ways to diffuse or sidestep the question. For example, you might say, "I understand why you are raising the question but…" (and go on with what you want to say) Never let yourself be trapped into an argument. Everyone loses in that situation, but as a firm wanting the business you have the most to lose.

18. Large and Small Proposals: The Difference

The major difference in a large or small proposal is the number of people involved in the preparation of the proposal. Proposals are usually organized into sections. For example, one section may be the mandatory requirements, another the previous experience and another the work methodology. Different people will work on each of them.

Large Proposal:

The key to managing a large proposal is coordination. To name only some of the participants, there may be writers and technical experts for various sections, graphics, layout, costing and co-ordination of sub-contractors.

This means that a Proposal Manager coordinates, not controls. Much of the time will be spent with internal communications between parties. The one party that the Proposal Manager will have the least contact with is the Red Team. There will be the need for some discussion to clarify their comments and to let them know when work will be sent to them. However, their independence has to be maintained so a fire-wall (even if only mentally) has to be constructed between the Proposal Manager and the Red Team.

Once the proposal is ready, the problem then becomes production. This probably involves people producing charts, graphics and illustrations to support your information. This presents its own problems in coordination and in producing a final copy.

When it is ready, the difficulty is still not over. Often a large proposal is multi-volume. This means many people are working to produce the final product. There is the danger of missing sections or important documents.

I can recall reviewing a large multi-million dollar proposal that had at least five 3" binders of information. The mandatory requirements were very clear. A certain number of qualified personnel had to be offered. In order to prove they were qualified, a diploma for a technical course had to be submitted for every person offered. When the proposals were evaluated, it was discovered that the firm failed to provide one diploma for one person. As a mandatory condition of bidding, the firm was non-responsive. It is a sad comment that the firm could have won a bid worth over $20 million dollars. There is no way of knowing if they would have been the successful firm but only five bids were received and only three passed the initial evaluation stage of the mandatory requirements.

Small Proposal:

With a small proposal there may only be two or three people involved. For example, the Proposal Manager may also be writing the proposal, creating the graphics, and doing the layout. There is no-one that they can turn to for advice or help.

At times, although this is never recommended, they also perform the Red Team role. This situation is discussed in a separate section.

Once the proposal is produced, it is assembled and sent to a printer. Conversely, it may be printed or photocopied in-house. In either case, assembly has to be carefully checked and re-checked to ensure no errors.

19. Alternate Proposals

When writing a proposal, it is not unusual to discover that you have two or more possible alternate solutions for the client's need. When this occurs, you have to consider whether you should submit more than one or two proposals.

Under no circumstances should you propose more than two proposals. You are considered an expert in your field and should be able to recommend the best course of action. Too many alternate proposals is an indication that you are "playing it safe" and "don't know your own business".

There are both pros and cons to the dilemma of multiple proposals. A general rule is not to submit multiple proposals unless they are specifically requested. If you ever decide to submit more than one proposal, do not try and produce your proposal in two sections. Instead, submit two completely different proposals even though this means duplicating information.

The Cons:
- Requires much more work for your firm resulting in two proposals of reduced quality.
- Requires you to divide scarce people resources instead of everyone working together.
- Customer may not appreciate having to evaluate two proposals.
- Creates double the workload for the customer.
- May give the impression that you don't know how to do the job.
- The alternate proposal may be unacceptable which would cause the customer to question your abilities on the acceptable proposal.
- The customer doesn't want or need the alternative since the alternative does not match the evaluation criteria.

The Pros:
- Providing the service in multiple locations may be more cost effective if the service is provided from one location or, alternately, may be more cost effective if the service is provided from multiple locations.

The Exception that proves the Rule:
- The RFP specifically suggests alternate proposals and advises how they are to be presented.
- The RFP is very poorly written and you are forced to make competing assumptions regarding what is required.
- The RFP advises that you can bid on some or all of the elements of the RFP and advised how the separate evaluations will be done.

20. Incumbents Disadvantage

Just as the name implies, The Incumbent's Disadvantage is a situation that only the incumbent contractor faces. It is not a well known or recognized term or situation. The only firm affected by this "disease" is the firm presently doing the work.

There are two possible symptoms, either of which can be fatal, for winning the right to continue working with the client.

The first symptom reflects that incumbent suppliers may have too much knowledge of the client's needs. In writing their proposal, they may relax how they write. They often think, "They know what we mean." meaning that they believer the evaluators will understand their written word without the need to be specific or detailed.

Written proposals are normally evaluated only on what is written. The best rule of thumb is to write all requirements down. Whether or not the client knows what is meant, they should be able to read the explanation.

The second symptom is that the incumbent supplier believes that they already know the client's needs in depth. In producing the proposal, the supplier eliminates possible alternatives, options or innovative solutions. In other words, they produce a proposal that is self-limiting. The explanation is that the customer won't or can't accept new or alternative ideas anyway. This is an understandable assumption that stems from working closely with a customer but it is a mistake.

Never take it for granted that you have to do less than your best or limit yourself when submitting a proposal. You do not know who the evaluators are (even if you think you do) and evaluators cannot use knowledge in their head. The written word governs.

How to Respond to a RFP
Winning Proposal Writing

21. Proposal Preparation: Outsourcing

With the complexity of bidding increasing every year, it costs firms more and more to bid. Proposals are costly to prepare. This includes the hidden costs – the cost of the time employees of the firm spend working on (or discussing and thinking about) the proposal, and the lost opportunity cost of not working on more productive endeavours.

The option of doing less than your best is not an option. It is better not to bid at all than to prepare an inferior bid. This is especially important to Government contractors, because a large effort is often required to prepare winning proposals. With the large effort required, more firms are hiring outside expertise – firms that are experts in the analysis of bids and proposal preparation.

To make the determination whether to hire outside resources or prepare your own proposals, firms have to analyze their own situation. Factors in this decision are:
- The firm's goals. If they are determined to expand and grow considerably, then having a higher percentage success in winning bids is essential.
- The effort that will be needed to get the bids prepared.
- Whether the firm will be bidding on more small contracts so that it can handle all the proposal work in-house
- Whether the firm will be bidding on larger more complex requirements that require more assistance.

Most companies fall in between the two extremes and use a mixture of in-house resources and consultants. Whether the proposal should be outsourced, in-house or a combination of the two depends on the needs of the firm.

Permanent Staff

Companies are faced with the dilemma of whether to use permanent staff or to hire specialized proposal writers. If you are bidding on a large number of smaller RFPs, and the RFPs are extremely similar to each other, you may have developed sufficient in-house expertise to handle all your proposals. In the event that there is an opportunity to bid on an exceptionally large dollar value RFP, you still have the option of hiring outside expertise to assist.

There may also be other considerations of importance such as the firm having valuable trade secrets that would be compromised by using consultant personnel.

As a business decision, you may choose not to outsource. Confidentiality and long term vision may mean that your goals can be achieved only with permanent staff. On the flip side, this may mean that you have fewer resources to devote to proposal development on bids that you could win.

Outsourcing

A firm that responds to RFPs infrequently or at irregular intervals is probably better off hiring some outside expertise to prepare its bids. This applies to firms of all sizes. The question becomes if all, or part, of the proposal development should be outsourced.

There are a number of options:
a. outsource the complete work
b. outsource the writing and layout
c. outsource the "Red Team" function only

Proposal Preparation - Outsourcing

For any solution, the core of a responsive proposal is the technical approach. An outside writer will need your subject matter specialists to provide the technical information for them to write the proposed solution. Outside writers can develop an outline for your subject matter specialists to follow but they usually cannot write those critical, convincing sections of the proposed solution that are frequently the difference between winning and losing.

In the unlikely event that you do not have a "subject matter" expert, this can be out-sourced as well.

Often, while firms are technically competent, they do not have a professional writer available or on staff. The outside expertise again is of value. They know how to write and present a proposal that will meet evaluators' expectations.

Although, it appears that a large firm would have the in-house resources, RFPs may arrive when staff is fully committed elsewhere. In fact, two or more RFPs could arrive at the same time.

It may also be the case that a larger firm bids only infrequently on RFPs and doesn't have the expertise at all. Regardless, since RFPs can differ, any firm may lack the expertise and understanding needed in regard to the procurement process, its dynamics and evaluations. In such situations, firms should consider hiring outside help to improve the quality of the proposal and the odds of winning.

There is a limited number of firms with in-depth proposal writing expertise. There is also a trend towards placing one or more experts on a retainer basis. This serves two purposes. The first is that the experts can now work more closely with your firm to understand your business. The second is exclusivity. As long as they work with you, they are obligated not to work with your competitors.

22. Public Sector vs. Private Industry - a Comparison

The Procurement Process: In Brief

There are two distinct marketplaces. While many companies do business almost exclusively with the public sector, many other companies do business almost exclusively with the private sector. Whether public sector or private industry, the competitive procurement process is essentially the same for complex requirements.

It is well worth keeping in mind that the term "RFP" is used in a generic fashion. Although the legal and operational situations differ between RFSA (Request for Supply Arrangement), RFSO (Request for Standing Offers) and RFP (Request for Proposal), the bidding and evaluation situation is virtually identical.

The Public Sector RFPs tend to be more complex due to the "public' nature. Due to the differences in the operating dynamics between the two, the following description of the process is written primarily from the point of view of the public sector. The rationale behind this decision is that the public sector procedures are more stringent and restrictive due to their accountability framework. Every decision can be challenged by taxpayers, including firms who pay taxes and by politicians and media. Private industry does not have this type of accountability. Private industry is generally accountable to the directors and the shareholders. Therefore decisions are made much quicker to work with firms that they know rather than offering the opportunity to every firm who wants to bid.

How to Respond to a RFP
Winning Proposal Writing

The process starts with development of a Statement of Work (Requirement) that describes a good or service that is needed.

Next, a RFP is developed. Every RFP is unique and complex. In the public sector, they are normally long with an overabundance of boilerplate clauses. This is done to remove all risk from the procurement process. In contrast, private industry tends to have shorter, more concise RFPs. They also require shorter proposals. The risk is greater but private industry makes decisions quicker. As stated above, they are accountable to their directors and shareholders, not to every taxpayer.

The next step is for the proposals received to be evaluated. This is done by a formal evaluation committee using a point scoring scheme. The difficulty from the viewpoint of the evaluators is to eliminate subjectivity. In the end, the decision is supposed to be objective. This is why previous knowledge or experience with the firm is not allowed, unless otherwise stated. The judgment is totally on the written word. Again, private industry often deviates from this rule. They would prefer to work with a supplier who has a proven track record at a higher cost, than a new supplier who they do not know well and whose cost is lower.

Due to the above, public sector proposal writing is much more difficult. They are often described as being a "brick". In other words long, in-depth, and covering every possibility. Firms bidding have to meet all requirements (mandatory and evaluated) or they are eliminated. Even proven performers have to pass this hurdle on new requirements. The private sector varies on this practice. Large firms come close to the public sector structure. Medium size and smaller firms normally want shorter proposals. Unlike the public sector, they do not have the resources to devote to evaluating large complicated proposals.

It is interesting that when bidding for the public sector, customers are defined as the Project Authorities (the ones in charge with and affected by implementation) by both bidding firms and the buyers. The customer could also be defined as another department or agency. In fact, generally, the entity that is funding the requirement is the considered the customer. In the public sector, for the most part, the supplier/customer relationship is not considered of major importance. The procurement process is considered paramount.

On the other hand, in the private sector, bidding firms define customers as the buyers. The internal clients (project authorities) are normally considered to play a supporting role. This means that the supplier/customer relationship is considered important. The procurement process is considered important but it is more important to ensure that you can work with the winner than to have the "best qualified" firm through a written evaluation.

It is important to remember that the goal of the public sector organization and the private industry firm is the same. Both ultimately want high quality products or services that meet their need at a fair price.

Public Sector

The Public Sector is large but has the advantage of having a rigid bidding structure regardless of the level of government – federal, provincial, municipal – or the type of public sector organization – government, agency, commission, etc. Many firms do very well bidding only in response to public sector RFPs. While the process is generally much more complicated and time consuming than for the private sector, it also has processes, rules and regulations that structure the bidding in a manner that is fair to all bidders.

The advantage of doing business with the public sector is that, although complicated and different for each government or agency, their processes are regulated. The public sector has constant criteria. A public sector RFP contains a SOW (Statement of Work) instruction on how to format your proposal (evaluation criteria) and how the scoring and selection process will be done.

Unlike private industry which can address needs by selecting bidders or choosing one firm to negotiate with, the public sector has to consider openness and transparency.

Every procurement action is governed by accountability to the public. This means that all procurement files must be well documented as procurement officers are accountable for every decision. A politician, auditor, or unsuccessful firm can question results and each decision has to be explainable and provable. Therefore public procurements proceed under the concepts of prudence (be careful) and probity (do it right).

The underlying rationale for this is that bidders are taxpayers. Taxpayers have rights. When you pay taxes, the assumption is that you have rights with regard to how your taxes are spent. For a business, this translates into the right to bid on procurements that their taxes help pay for. It also translates into the right of a taxpayer to ensure that public funds (ie. their money) were spent properly, which is why a bid can be challenged.

Public Sector Procurement Structure

As stated, the government uses procurement processes that are highly structured. They appear to be complex with an overabundance of rules and regulations. Public sector RFPs are long, full of boilerplate terms and conditions and contain a structure that guides the bidder in preparing a proposal. There is normally a Statement of Work, evaluation criteria with the scoring, the terms and conditions that a bidder must follow, how the proposal should be structured and possibly a draft of terms that will be part of the contract.

Public Sector vs. Private Industry – a Comparison

Private sector RFPs, in contrast, may not be written clearly, not be well organized and may leave important terms and conditions to be negotiated later. Public sector RFPs are rigid and a formal team is struck to evaluate proposals. In contrast, the private sector may have only one or two people review the proposals.

The other important item of consideration is that for Public Sector RFPs, the closing time for the bid is fixed. If you deliver even one minute late, your bid will not be considered. A recommendation is for a bidder to ship the proposal by two different methods. In this way if only one bid arrives on time, it will be considered responsive. The second bid will be considered a confirmation of the earlier bid.

For the public sector, the relationship with the customer is secondary to the process that determines who will win. In fact, with rare exceptions, in the public sector, prior knowledge of firms and relationships is not allowed to enter into the evaluation. The evaluation is done strictly on the written submission.

In the last ten to fifteen years the bidding process has evolved. Public sector organizations used to create and maintain lists of potential suppliers. Considerable resources were devoted to this endeavour as there are literally thousands of potential suppliers. When a bid opportunity came, a RFP was sent to firms on the list.

This has changed. Many private industry firms and some public sector organizations still maintain these lists. Most public sector organizations now post large bidding opportunities on an electronic bulletin board. This advertises the bidding opportunity to all firms.

It is up to the firm to decide if they are interested in or capable of supplying the good or service that is advertised. In this way, instead of the organization pre-qualifying firms and maintaining source lists, potential bidders now have to pre-qualify themselves against every potential opportunity.

Using an electronic bulletin board has caused a major change in the creation of RFPs. Buyers want to evaluate as few bids as possible. When source lists were used this could be ensured. With electronic bulletin boards and firms doing their own screening, a bid opportunity is potentially open to hundreds of bids. To control this, restricting criteria such as previous projects or years of experience will be used. Thus, to ensure only a limited number of bids are received, the evaluation criteria are carefully thought out.

Private sector organizations are gradually following. This is one of the few times that the public sector has been the innovator with the private sector following.

If you understand the public sector procedures and have the discipline required to bid on RFPs, you can adapt to the requirements of the private sector. The converse is not true. In a business proposal, you can be as non-compliant as you want and, if innovative, still might receive the contract.

Request For Information (RFI)

For large complex requirements, the Public Sector often use a RFI to explore the possibility of competitive bidding or improvements in a forthcoming requirement.

The public sector will issue the RFI by the electronic bulletin board so that all potential bidders can see the request. The RFI will highlight in detail the need of the client and ask for input. This need could range from an outline of a Statement of Work to a complete draft RFP. Firms interested in bidding on the eventual RFP are requested to respond with recommendations.

Public Sector vs. Private Industry – a Comparison

From the viewpoint of a bidder, this may be an opportunity to have the requirement defined in a way that is an advantage to the bidder. On the other hand, any recommendation used will be known to everyone which may be an advantage to a competitor.

Careful consideration is required as to whether to respond to a RFI. On the one hand, it has the advantage of making your firm known to the eventual client. On the other hand, it requires time and effort to develop a reply that will not be paid for.

Private Industry

In contrast to the public sector, private industry generally has a different approach. For the most part, private industry still uses source lists in a competitive bidding situation.

The competitive process is not as structured as in the public sector. Companies in the private sector often have less formality in the proposal processes and have much less consistency between RFPs. There are few regulations that are imposed on their process. In fact, there may be no detailed written RFP for your proposal to be evaluated against and even no defined SOW. There may be only an "idea" and an outline of the idea.

It is harder to use boilerplates and the proposal requirements vary considerably depending on the firm issuing the RFP. With only self-imposed regulations the firm may phone for clarifications regarding any proposal received, whether compliant or non-compliant.

In the private sector, the relationship with the customer can be more important than the document. If they know a firm that is bidding (relationship), they may require the proposal to be reworked even if there are other firms also bidding. The closing date, for example, is not rigid. By phoning, even at the last minute, a short extension of an hour or two can often be arranged.

Previous relationships, the bidder's credentials and reputation, can and are factored into the assessment. The lowest bid from an unknown firm may not be selected. Should proposals and prices be reasonably close, a higher priced bid (with lower written quality) may be selected if the customer knows the firm and has confidence that the quality of work that will be done by the bidder was not reflected in the proposal.

In this way, a firm that is known and is technically non-compliant (having missed information defined as mandatory) may still be considered for and awarded a contract.

Proposals that are written for private industry generally reward innovation. This means that if you have an excellent idea, you can be non-compliant with the evaluation criteria and still win the contract.

The private sector RFP is often nebulous with limited details. It may be that most of the information has been provided through earlier meetings and you have been asked to write a proposal based on these meetings. The proposal that you prepare will probably have a limited number of pages. However, it should have similar elements to the public sector. In other words it should have an outline, a statement of the work to be done, how that work will be addressed and milestones, payment details, delivery, etc.

In private industry the proposal may have been won even before the competitive RFP was issued. Again, the relationship with and knowledge of the customer is important. The proposal is still important. A poorly written proposal is an indicator that the bidder does not take the work seriously and/or takes the relationship for granted. A well written proposal indicates that,

Public Sector vs. Private Industry – a Comparison

even though you have an excellent relationship with the customer, you are not taking him/her for granted and that your firm takes pride in demonstrating its excellence in all matters – the end product and the proposal.

Probably the major distinction between the public sector and private industry is how pricing is treated. The public sector splits the proposal into two – pricing and technical. The evaluators do the technical evaluation without knowing the pricing as this could affect their decisions. They might, for example, penalize a firm unfairly in their evaluation if they saw their price by believing the solution wouldn't work since the price is too low. Private Industry often takes a different approach. The two are often combined and the evaluators start with looking at the price. "Can they afford it?" may be the first question asked. Why read and evaluate a proposal that they can't afford.

As private sector firms become larger, issue stock and become more accountable to shareholders, their procedures grow and develop. With the resulting increase in the dollar value and complexity of the procurement processes in private industry, the need for a much more complicated RFP develops and complex evaluation methodology emerges. The result is that the private industry procurement process adopts many of the public sector procedures and becomes closer to the public sector process. It is rare, though, that the RFP becomes as complex or as rigid in its evaluation as with the public sector

Even though the structure is different, the lessons learned from preparing proposals for the public sector is a major asset. It is far easier to write in an unstructured environment using the tools learned in a highly structured environment. The ability to write proposals for the public sector makes it much easier to write superior proposals for the private sector

How to Respond to a RFP
Winning Proposal Writing

Strategic Alliance

A strategic alliance in simple terms is two or more firms working together to accomplish a goal that neither could on their own. This is also often called a joint venture. In a strategic alliance the parties accept risk and reward for the success or failure of the project. There should be a contract signed by all parties describing their roles and the profit sharing arrangements.

While the same goal can be accomplished through sub-contractor arrangements, the RFP may prohibit this possibility. For example, the RFP evaluation may require the bidder to have certain experience or to have accomplished similar projects. You can have two firms, neither of which can meet the full requirement but taking their joint experience they meet and exceed the evaluation requirement. A bid by one using the other as sub-contractor would not work in this case as the evaluation criteria stated the bidder has to have the experience. The solution is to form a strategic alliance, to prepare a joint proposal and submit the proposal as a joint venture. In this way the experience of both firms becomes valid they are considered to be one bidder to the RFP.

Care must be taken in these situations. You are creating a partnership when you bid this way and normally you are liable for the work even if the other member of the strategic alliance fails to fulfill their obligations.

One alternative is to form a new legal entity or corporation to bid on the RFP. This has its own drawbacks. Normally it takes more time to incorporate than the bidding period would allow. Also, you may face expensive legal fees.

How to Respond to a RFP
Winning Proposal Writing

Subcontractors

Often firms employ subcontractors to write and develop a proposal. That is discussed in another section.

If you are not going to form a strategic alliance or a joint venture with another firm, you have to decide how to proceed. Large requirements are normally beyond the ability of any one firm to handle. Firms do not have permanent staff sitting around waiting for work. Instead they contract expertise to provide support services or missing capabilities as needed.

Under these circumstances, you are faced with two alternatives if you want to work on the resulting work from the RFP. Either you have subcontractors or you become a subcontractor.

Using a Subcontractor

Many firms know and use the same pool of subcontractors continually. Reliable and known subcontractors are the ideal. Subcontractors are not always available and there is always a need to find more.

If an electronic bulletin board is being used for the RFP, the list of potential bidders may be available. This is an ideal place to look. Small firms, unable to bid on their own, may have requested the bid documents. An examination of the list should indicate two or three potential small firms to approach.

When preparing the proposal, the one thing that you should plan on is that subcontractors will be late providing any information that you request. Moreover, the information that you have requested will usually contain omissions and need formatting work on your part to incorporate them into the proposal.

The Proposal Manager has to treat subcontractors differently. You have to be clear with them as to your expectations, including deadlines. There has to be continual follow-ups done to get the information. If five subcontractors are required to do a particular service, it is recommended that the Proposal Manager (or his delegate) work with more subcontractors than the required number (five). In this way your proposal will not be in jeopardy if one does not supply the information on time.

Each subcontractor has to commit to working with you (in writing preferably). You can then state this in your proposal. However, reality does set in. You are bidding to win, not to do the job. The subcontractors that you use to win the bid may not be available by the time the evaluation is done and the contract is awarded. Plan on replacements.

Being a Subcontractor

It takes time and dedication to prepare a proposal. Whether your firm is just starting out or is an established firm with a proven track record, you have to decide if you are going to bid on a RFP or not. The Bid/No-Bid evaluation will help you with this determination.

Supposing the result of the Bid/No Bid evaluation is a recommendation that you don't bid due to the need to have subcontractors. In that event, you still have an avenue open to you. You can approach another firm, that is bidding, to become their subcontractor.

As mentioned before, if an electronic bulletin board is being used for the RFP, the list of potential bidders may be available. This is an ideal place to look for a firm.

There may also be firms that you have worked for in the past and with whom you have a good relationship. I have had the occasion to approach a firm that could bid with knowledge of the requirement. I knew that I had the missing piece of expertise that was needed for them to bid. They prepared and submitted the proposal.

When you become a subcontractor ensure that you are never late in providing any information that is requested. You may even offer to help write the proposal if that is appropriate. Your goal is to establish your firm as a reputable firm that will be asked to participate as a subcontractor in future RFPs.

Another advantage to becoming a subcontractor is that you are able to learn on the job. As your firm grows and develops, you will see more opportunities than you can participate in. As a subcontractor, you can also learn how contracts with subcontractors should work. Eventually you may prepare your own proposals and bid directly

How to Respond to a RFP
Winning Proposal Writing

Appendix A - Letters

No Bid Letters

Example 1:

Dear,

This is written in regard to your recent RFP for quality management services.

Unfortunately circumstances have prevented us from bidding at this time. We are already busy on other major projects and do not have the experienced resources available for your requirement at this time.

Should you receive no qualified bids, we would be willing to reconsider this decision and try to reallocate or employ sufficient additional resources

In any event, please keep us in mind for future requirements.

Yours sincerely,

(Note: The letter does not go into details. The goal is to be positive and make the client aware that your firm is available and willing to help out.)

Example 2:

Dear,

We have examined your RFP for quality management services closely. Due to the requirement for 75 full time employees, we are unable to bid. Our firm has only 40 full time employees.

As we are expanding our workforce, this situation should change in the near future and we then would welcome the opportunity to submit a proposal.

Yours truly,

(Note: The goal in the above two letters is the same although the wording is different. In the letter above you are alerting the client to the reason that caused your decision to not bid on their RFP.)

Appendix B The Top Ten
(Useful Checklists)

The Top 10 Reviewing a RFP

1. Can you meet the Statement of Work/Requirement Definition?
2. Is the RFP biased towards one firm.
3. Do you need to involve outside resources? In other words, sub-contractors.
4. Is the RFP clearly written? Do you understand what is required?
5. Can you meet the Mandatory Requirements?
6. Can you meet the Rated Requirements?
7. Is the Delivery Date or Date of Completion reasonable?
8. Are there questions that need to be answered regarding the RFP?
9. Have you created a timeline for preparing the Proposal response?
10. Is there contradictory information contained in the RFP?

The Top Ten When Preparing a Proposal Do...

1. Write what the customer says that they want, not what they actually need.
2. Write complete responses to the evaluation criteria addressing the criteria as they are written. Do not be creative.
3. Ensure that each and every item that is to be evaluated is answered.
4. For mandatory requirements, start your statement with words similar to, "We fully meet the criteria...." The evaluators are then left with either agreeing with you or disagreeing with you

and having to give reasons for their decision. Don't leave decisions open for the evaluator to make.
5. Write in a clear, concise manner.
6. Ensure that resumes are relevant to the qualifications needed and that they fully prove that the person is qualified (in accordance with the evaluation criteria)
7. Do not ramble or present material that is not pertinent. Evaluators may take it as an indicator on how you will perform the work. Good proposals are generally written by firms who are good contractors.
8. Customize your description of your corporate qualifications to the requirement of the RFP. Ensure that there is sufficient depth and that all details relate to the RFP requirement.
9. Do not directly compare yourself to your competitors. If you are aware of weaknesses of your competitors, you can write an advisement into your bid stating that you fully meet the requirement in the area where you believe that they are weak.
10. Try and sound unique. (It can be done). What makes you special and why should they pick you. At the same time, you still have to meet the evaluation criteria.

The Top Ten When Preparing a Proposal Don't...

1. Assume that you know better than the customer. You may have the expertise but the customer is the one who is defining the need.
2. Add resumes and company profiles for show. Meaningful content will get better results than puffery.
3. Use boilerplates unless you customize them to the client's stated needs.
4. Boast. Boasting is meaningless. Prove what you say.
5. Choose formats, fonts, styles, graphics for show. It is important that the proposal can be read and understood.

Appendix B – The Top Ten

6. Use long-winded sentences with "fancy" words. Write short sentence and paragraphs in easy to understand language.
7. Use technical jargon without explaining the meaning of the words or phrases. Not all evaluators are technical experts.
8. Write a chapter when a paragraph would do. Evaluators are looking for clear explanations, not long-winded ones that confuse rather than explain.
9. Delay redrafting sections of the proposal until all the sections have been assembled.
10. Photocopy if you can print. Large and small proposals have been ruled non-compliant when pages have become stuck together in photocopying. The resulting proposals had critical information missing so had to be judged non-compliant.

The Top Ten What Evaluators Want

1. That bidders answer only what the RFP requests.
2. That all evaluation criteria are met and there is a clear statement that they are met.
3. That there is no eulogizing. Extra unnecessary reading is not appreciated.
4. That the proposal is clear. Using short, to the point explanations.
5. That boilerplate materials are used carefully with the content relevant and with only minor customizations.
6. That brochures and marketing information are not attached that have nothing to do with the RFP.
7. That the personnel who are doing the work have the skills and expertise and this is supported in their resumes or other written material.
8. That the bidder can meet the schedule and has given details and milestones.
9. That they do not assume they know what the client wanted.
10. That bidders remember their proposals are not a work of fiction or unnecessary self-promotion.

The Top Ten Major Mistakes in preparing a Proposal

The most common mistakes in preparing a proposal tend to be repeated over and over again. Whether a large company or a small company, mistakes happen. They can be as simple as forgetting to sign the proposal thereby invalidating it, or inadvertently dropping sections. The list below will help you avoid the most common mistakes.

1. Not doing a Bid/No Bid Analysis

The expression, "Fools rush in where angels fear to tread", is very true. Firms obtain a copy of the RFP, look at it quickly and start working on their proposal immediately. They do not take the time to consider the number of potential bidders (ie. the competition) or whether there are major roadblocks that prevent them from bidding. They spend their limited resources working hard, often with overtime, on a bid with little chance of success.

More than once the Proposal Manager has told me that the only reason that they are working on a certain proposal was orders from higher management who want to be seen to being active.

2. Not starting work immediately

Another large failing is assuming that there is plenty of time to prepare the proposal. The RFP is put aside due to "more important work" and not actioned immediately. The result is there is no opportunity to ask and obtain answers to critical questions. In the case of the incumbent contractor, I have seen firms run out of time and be unable to submit a proposal at all. They thought they knew what the client wanted until they finally read the RFP.

Appendix B – The Top Ten

3. Not meeting the Mandatory Requirements

Invariably, whether I review bids for clients or evaluate proposals for clients, the same main mistake occurs. They fail to meet all the mandatory requirements specified in the RFP. From a bidder's viewpoint, they might just as well have not bid. If you do not take the time to ensure that you meet (or can meet) the mandatory requirements, then you have wasted your valuable resources time and effort.

On one large, multimillion dollar contract, no bidder met the mandatory requirements. The two best firms in the industry both omitted a mandatory section by accident. They were different sections but the fact remained that a rebid was necessary. Had either of the firms met the mandatory requirements with their proposal, they would have won the contract. Try telling that to the firm that ended up losing the bid. There is no consolation prize.

4. Assuming evaluators know what they are evaluating

Usually you don't know who will be doing the evaluation. It is a mistake to assume that evaluators are technical experts. It is also a mistake to assume that evaluators know how to evaluate. There are many instances where evaluators who are not subject matter experts are deliberately used. Part of the rationale is that anyone should be able to understand concepts easily. Using trade jargon that only people with inside knowledge "might" understand can be, and has been, used as a means to disguise a lack of understanding by the bidder.

5. Not following the RFP guidelines

It is not enough to follow the Scope of Work (Requirements Definition or Statement of Requirements) line by line. The bidder must not just focus on proving that they can do all the elements in the Scope of Work. The rated evaluation may contain other elements that must be responded to. To ignore these elements is to risk not meeting the proposal requirements

If a bidder cannot read and understand a RFP correctly, the firm is judged as unable to do the work correctly, and the bid fails. Structure your proposal in the manner that the RFP requests. Follow this structure closely through all cross references, etc. It is recommended that you number your proposal response exactly with the numbering scheme outlined in the RFP (if it has one) for the evaluation criteria.

6. Not looking for the Hidden Mandatory Requirements

Firms prepare proposals based on the listed mandatory and rated evaluation criteria. They often do not look through the proposal for the Hidden Mandatory Requirements. Considerable time and effort is put into developing the proposal only fail to meet a critical requirement, such as obtaining certifications from sub-contractors, meet security requirements, or even deliveries. Often a bidder will only realize this when the contract has been awarded and they are being debriefed on the bid.

This is why the Red Team concept is important. Part of their function is to review the RFP in total and highlight these requirements early in the process.

7. Focusing the Proposal on themselves rather than the client

It is essential that the bidder informs evaluators what they can do. However, some firms take the attitude that we know better than the client. They don't focus on addressing the client's expressed needs. Sentences will continually start with a "we" focus. They should have a "you" or customer focus. For example a statement such as, "We will do ...since that is our core business." instead of "In support of your needs, we will do..."

Over the years, I have evaluated many proposals where the first one third of the proposal (many pages) is about the firm, its experience, its people, its range of projects, etc. Not one word of this was linked to the RFP that was under evaluation. The Executive Summary should be 1 to 2 pages long, not book length. If you want to add brochures or literature, insert them as an Appendix.

Focus your proposal on the client, not on your firm.

8. A bidder assuming that they will win the RFP, not that they have to earn the contract

This has been discussed elsewhere and is part of the Incumbent's Dilemma. It is also a problem faced by a firm that has worked closely with the client on other projects.

Don't take anything for granted. Write to win as if the client has never heard about your firm before.

9. Trying for a Pass, not 100%

This is another common failing in the competitive bid process. Regardless of the method of evaluation used, I have had it said to me many times, "We only need 70% to pass" or "We only need 80% to pass." The only difference between those statements and others is the pass mark. The fact remains a firm that works for a pass can easily not win the bid. There are two good reasons for this.

First, you do not know who the evaluator's are. Working for a pass, can result in a score below the threshold. It is easy to overlook an element or downplay an element that is important in the evaluator's mind.

Second, with a low score, you will find that a firm who works harder to gain the marks ends up with a higher overall assessment and wins the bid.

Surprisingly, this statement holds true for evaluations based on lowest price responsive proposal method. In this method, all firms who pass are considered equal. The winning bid is then the lowest priced bid of those who passed. Although the bids become equal before price is considered, a firm who paid more attention to the score and obtained a higher mark, is often a firm that paid more attention to the price and submitted a lower price, thereby winning the bid.

10. Bidding to do the job, not bidding to win the right to do the job

I cannot count the number of discussions that I have had with various firms with regard to assisting them to develop their proposal. A common statement made is, "But that is not what they need?", when referring to the client's requirement.

Some bidders never seem to realize that there is a difference between bidding to do the job and bidding to win the right to do the job. Admittedly, you want to do job. But, if you don't win the contract, you won't be able to do the job. Your proposal must be written to respond to the RFP and win the contract. Once you have won the contract, you will be in a position to dialogue directly with the client and suggest improvements.

Appendix C Case Study

A RFP Example

The following is an example bid to help you understand and analyze a relatively complex RFP process. The term RFP is still used in its general sense to describe the process although the actual bid document that will be analyzed was a Request for Supply Arrangement (RFSA).

This document was actually used in the format presented. Changes have been made to names, numbers and subject matter.

Although the headers have been left intact, there are considerable deletions regarding the boilerplate content used in RFPs by the customer. This is not to imply that the content is not important. From a bidding viewpoint, it is extremely important to understand all the legal clauses in a RFP. However, you will find it relevant to realize how much of a RFP consists of boilerplate type clauses.

For the purpose of understanding how to respond to a RFP, the focus is on clauses that affect the evaluation and the resulting outcome of the RFP process. The commentary in italics was not part of the original RFP and has been inserted to help you to understand it. As always, it is recommended that the RFP be read in the following order:
- The Statement of Work
- The evaluation criteria
- The rest of the RFP

The original RFP was 23,446 words long or about one half the length of this complete book.

REQUEST FOR SUPPLY ARRANGEMENT (RFSA) FOR RISK MANAGEMENT SERVICES

The purpose of this Request for Supply Arrangement (RFSA) is to establish, with up to five (5) qualified Risk Management Service Providers, Supply Arrangements to assist business lines, processes and operations to achieve measurable risk management improvements, by utilizing methodologies associated with risk management on an "as, when and if requested basis".

This opening statement has important information. The customer intends to qualify up to five firms as a result of the RFP process. This has major implications for the Bid/No Bid analysis.

This procurement vehicle has two stages; Stage 1 may result in the issuance of Supply Arrangements to Offeror(s), and Stage 2 may result in the issuance of a contract(s) to a Supply Arrangement Holder, for specific professional services to be provided to an authorized client in the Department of Status Quo.

More important information is being conveyed. The original bid (this document) will not result in work. Instead, it will result in the opportunity for work in the future.

The period of a Supply Arrangement(s) will be from date of issuance of a SA **for a three (3) year period, with three (3) one (1) year option periods**.

This is another important item. Should you bid on this RFSA and be successful, you and four other firms (maximum) will have the opportunity to have 'exclusive' work for up to six years.

This document is divided into Parts and Sections.
(customer boilerplate not shown)

Appendix C – Case Study

Part "1" provides general information on "How to" make your offer to CRA.
(customer boilerplate not shown)
Part "2" includes a Model Supply Arrangement
(customer boilerplate not shown)

Table of Contents

PART 1 – INFORMATION AND INSTRUCTIONS TO SUPPLIERS
Section I – General Information
(customer boilerplate not shown)
Section II– Instructions for Submitting an Offer
(customer boilerplate not shown)
Section III – Evaluation and Selection
(customer boilerplate not shown)
Section IV – Evaluation Criteria
(customer boilerplate not shown)

Section V – Financial Offer
(customer boilerplate not shown)
Annex A-1 to Part 1 Certifications Required To Be Submitted At Time Of Bid Closing
(customer boilerplate not shown)
Annex A-2 to Part 1 Certifications Required To Be Submitted Prior To SA Award
(customer boilerplate not shown)

PART 2 - MODEL SUPPLY ARRANGEMENT
Section I – General Information
(customer boilerplate not shown)
Section II – Statement of Work
(customer boilerplate not shown)
Section III – Solicitations Issued Against the Supply Arrangements for Stage 2
(customer boilerplate not shown)

Section IV - Resulting Contract Clauses, Terms and Conditions for Stage 2 of the Procurement Process
(customer boilerplate not shown)

Annex A Certifications Required To Be Submitted At Time of RFP Closing
(customer boilerplate not shown)

Annex B Security Requirements Check List (SRCL)
(customer boilerplate not shown)

Part "1" - Information and Instructions to Suppliers

SECTION I - GENERAL INFORMATION
(customer boilerplate not shown)

1.0 DEFINITIONS
(customer boilerplate not shown)

2.0 INTRODUCTION

The Department of Status Quo would like to develop a procurement vehicle by establishing up to five (5) Supply Arrangements with qualified Risk Management Providers, to assist business lines to achieve measurable risk improvements, by utilizing methodologies associated with risk management. Offerors are advised that this vehicle is one of a number of vehicles that the Agency will be using to meet its needs and that the Agency reserves the right to obtain services to satisfy its requirements outside the Supply Arrangements.

This is normally a reiteration of the purpose written at the beginning of the RFP. It is important to check that it is the same. In this case, the opening statement contains more information than the Introduction. This needs to be clarified, probably through a question to the purchasing authority.

Appendix C – Case Study

3.0 SUPPLY ARRANGEMENT METHOD OF PROCUREMENT

The intent of a SA is to establish a framework with a Supplier to permit the expeditious processing of legally binding contracts for the specified services.
(customer boilerplate not shown)

The SA is not in itself a Contract but rather, a framework that forms part of any resulting Request for Proposals (RFPs) and Contracts.
(customer boilerplate not shown)

4.0 OVERVIEW OF THE PROCUREMENT PROCESS

This RFSA represents the first of a two-stage procurement process
(customer boilerplate not shown)
This just reinforced information given in the introduction

Stage 1 - Request for Supply Arrangement (RFSA) Stage
Stage 1 will be the selection of the successful Offeror(s) for the RFSA. This will be achieved in
accordance with Section III titled 'Evaluation Selection'.
(customer boilerplate not shown)

Stage 2 - Contract Stage
For Stage 2, one or many SA Holders holding an applicable SA will be invited to submit a proposal under a Request for Proposal for that requirement. The SA Holders invited will be required to submit a detailed proposal, including a detailed résumé for each proposed resource.
This is important new information. The successful firms on the RFSA will still have to go through a RFP process to get work. In other words, you have to win this competitive process in order to be part of the competitive process for future work.

5.0 SUPPLY ARRANGEMENT RE-POSTING
The CRA reserves the right to post a notice on the Government Electronic Tendering Service (GETS) inviting new firms and existing Supply Arrangement Holders to submit offers should the SA Holders list contain less than five (5) SA Holders.
(customer boilerplate not shown)

6.0 APPLICABLE LAWS
(customer boilerplate not shown)

SECTION II - INSTRUCTIONS FOR SUBMITTING AN OFFER

1.0 OFFERS REQUESTED
(customer boilerplate not shown)

2.0 REVISION OF DEPARTMENTAL NAME
(customer boilerplate not shown)

3.0 STANDARD INSTRUCTIONS AND CONDITIONS
(customer boilerplate not shown)

4.0 ENQUIRIES WITH RESPECT TO THIS RFSA
(customer boilerplate not shown)

5.0 PREVIOUS COMMUNICATIONS BETWEEN GOVERNMENT AND OFFEROR
(customer boilerplate not shown)

6.0 AMENDMENTS TO THIS REQUEST FOR SUPPLY ARRANGEMENT
(customer boilerplate not shown)

7.0 AMENDMENTS TO OFFERORS' OFFERS
(customer boilerplate not shown)

Appendix C – Case Study

8.0 SUBMISSION OF OFFERS
(customer boilerplate not shown)

9.0 OFFER PREPARATION AND SUBMISSION INSTRUCTIONS
(customer boilerplate not shown)

PART I TECHNICAL OFFER
(customer boilerplate not shown)
The Offeror is requested to submit the original and **three (3) copies** of its technical offer.
This instructs the bidder as to the number of copies to submit.

PART II FINANCIAL OFFER
The Offeror shall provide ceiling per diem rates for the services requested in the Statement of Work, using the format outlined in Part 1, Section V: Financial Offer. These rates may be subject to downward revision only prior to issuance of a Contract. GST/HST is not to be included in the ceiling per diem rates. The Offeror shall submit an original of its financial offer.
This advises the bidders that prices are not firm but subject to downward revision. In other words, this is the first indication that the prices are ceiling prices. The number of copies of the financial proposal to be submitted are not specified. When details such as this are lacking the best assumption would be that the bidder should submit same number of copies as specified in the technical proposal - the original and three copies.

PART III CERTIFICATIONS
(customer boilerplate not shown)

10.0 WITHDRAWAL OF OFFER
(customer boilerplate not shown)

11.0 DEBRIEFING

(customer boilerplate not shown)

SECTION III - EVALUATION AND SELECTION

1.0 GENERAL
(customer boilerplate not shown)

2.0 STEPS IN THE EVALUATION AND SELECTION PROCESS
This is a vital section that details the exact evaluation process that will be used.

The selection process to determine the successful Offeror(s) will be carried out as follows:

2.1 Step 1 – Evaluation against Mandatory Criteria
Offers will be evaluated to determine if all the mandatory requirements detailed in Part 1, Section IV: Evaluation Criteria, 1.0 Mandatory Criteria, have been met. Only those offers meeting ALL mandatory requirements will then be evaluated in accordance with Step 2 below.
In other words, you have to succeed meet all the mandatory requirements to move to Step 2.

2.2 Step 2 – Evaluation against Point-Rated Criteria
Offers will be evaluated and scored in accordance with the point-rated evaluation criteria detailed herein, at Part 1, Section IV: Evaluation Criteria, 2.0 Point-Rated Technical Criteria. Any offer that does not achieve an overall minimum score of **70%** will be considered noncompliant and will receive no further consideration.
All offers meeting the minimum thresholds in Step 2 will proceed to Step 3.
In other words, you have to get at least 70% on the rated requirements in order to move to Step 3.

Appendix C – Case Study

2.3 Step 3 – Evaluation of Financial Offers

Only compliant offers meeting all of the requirements detailed in Steps 1 and 2 will be considered at this point. Prices submitted will be evaluated to determine the offer price score as defined herein, "Financial Offer". Failure or refusal to provide a price or rate for any item in Part 1, Section V: Financial Offer, shall be considered as failing to meet a mandatory requirement of the RFSA and therefore, the Offeror's offer shall be given no further consideration. Offerors must quote ceiling per diem rates in Canadian funds, GST or HST extra as applicable. Table V.1 will be used for the purposes of evaluating the Offeror's financial offer in accordance with the procedures outlined in Part 1, Section V: Financial Offer.

This is a complicated way of saying you have to pass steps 1and 2 to get to this point. Pricing is considered next.

2.4 Step 4 – Ranking of Offers
Highest Combined Rating of Technical Merit and Price Score

To determine an overall score for each offer, technical and price will each be given a rating value; in this case, **65%** for technical and **35%** for price, and then combined to derive a total combined rating. The scoring of technical merit will be derived by prorating the technical score on the point rated criteria against the stipulated total available points. The scoring of price will be derived by giving full marks to the lowest priced technically compliant offer and prorating all other compliant offers accordingly.

The following example illustrates how the total combined rating is determined using a ratio of 65% technical and 35% price:

Technical Score

Firm	Technical Points	Technical Score (65%)
A	620	620/1000 x 65= 40.30
B	650	650/1000 x 65 = 42.25
C	720	720/1000 x 65 = 46.80
D	790	790/1000 x 65 = 51.35
E	**960***	960/1000 x 65 = 62.40

Price Score

Firm	Offer Price	Price Score (35%)
A	**$500,000****	35.00
B	$520,000	$500,000/520,000 x 35 = 33.65
C	$580,000	$500,000/580,000 x 35 = 30.17
D	$700,000	$500,000/700,000 x 35 = 25.00
E	$2,000,000	$500,000/2,000,000 x 35 = 8.75

Total Combined Rating

Firm	Technical Score (65%)	Price Score (35%)	Total Combined Rating
A	40.30	35.00	75.30
B	42.25	33.65	75.90
C	46.80	30.17	**76.97***
D	51.35	25.00	76.35
E	62.40	8.75	71.15

Appendix C – Case Study

* highest scoring technically compliant offer
** highest scoring priced technically compliant offer
** highest scoring technically compliant offer
*** highest ranked offer

Offeror(s) meeting all the mandatory criteria and having obtained or exceeded the minimum pass mark within the point rated criteria will be ranked based on the highest Total Combined Rating of Technical Merit and Price Score. The top five (5) ranked Offerors will be awarded a Supply Arrangement.
This is well written and explains clearly how the technical score and the financial score will be combined. It clearly states that the top five firms in points will receive a Supply Arrangement.

2.5 Step 5 – Conditions Precedent to SA Entry
This section is simply more mandatory criteria, but not indentified as such earlier. In fact, they qualify as "hidden mandatory criteria".

2.5.1 Financial Capability
(customer boilerplate not shown)
2.5.2 Security Requirements
Personnel only – No Document Safeguarding Capability
(customer boilerplate not shown)
2.5.3 Insurance Requirements
(customer boilerplate not shown)
2.5.3.1 Errors and Omissions Liability Insurance
(customer boilerplate not shown)

SECTION IV – EVALUATION CRITERIA

1.0 MANDATORY CRITERIA
(customer boilerplate not shown)

1.1 MANDATORY TECHNICAL REQUIREMENTS

How to Respond to a RFP
Winning Proposal Writing

M1 The Offeror must provide summaries of five (5) projects completed within ten (10) years from the date of offer submission in the areas of process improvement services, where the Offeror was the primary contractor responsible for the projects. Each project summary must include the following information, as a minimum:
• A description of the project and how the process improvement services were utilized;
• A description of the process improvement methodology used;
• Duration of the project (start and end dates).
Information provided in the project summaries will be subject to validation by members of the evaluation team and will be used further at 2.0 Point Rated Evaluation Criteria. In order to validate the information, each referenced project must contain the following information:
1. Name of client organization.
2. Names, titles, telephone numbers, fax numbers and e-mail addresses of the primary and secondary client contacts.
Only **three (3)** attempts over a **maximum five (5) working-day period** from the first attempt to contact the reference will be made by the evaluators. If unsuccessful, the Offeror will be found non-compliant. Should discrepancies exist between the information submitted by the Offeror and the information provided by the contract reference, the information provided by the project reference will take precedence.

This requirement is a screening tool. New firms cannot meet the requirement and many firms will not have done five projects. The major concern to the bidder is the statement that the customer will make three attempts over five working days to contact the reference. If contact is not made, the bidder will be deemed non-compliant. In many ways this is an unfair situation. Your fate as a bidder is in the hands of one of your customers. Should there be a personal emergency for a reference, it is possible that your bid could be disqualified.

To address this potentially dangerous situation two things need to be done. The first is to ask your contact for a written reference

Appendix C – Case Study

that you will enclose with your bid. The second is to raise a question, on this restriction in the RFP, to the procurement authority.

M2 The Offeror must demonstrate it has a minimum of three (3) resources – each with experience in a minimum of three (3) risk management improvement projects in the last five (5) years. The Offeror must provide a resume for all proposed resources, clearly demonstrating where, when and how experience in process improvement was obtained.

This is unclear as there is no definition of resources. Does it mean that you must have permanent employees or does it mean that you must have access to a network of contractors to fill the need? As above, this is an item to raise as a question to the procurement authority.

M3 Each proposed resource must have, at minimum, an Undergraduate degree from a recognized University or a Diploma from a recognized College in one of the following: Business Administration, Accounting, Commerce, E-Business, Engineering or other comparable program. A copy of the degree or diploma must be submitted with the offer.

This is a good move to require a copy of the degree or diploma. However, in many cases extensive work experience and training can replace a degree. If you have an excellent person to offer who does not have a degree, it is recommended that you question the procurement authority whether a combination of post secondary and a specified number of years of appropriate experience would be considered the equivalent.

2.0 POINT RATED EVALUATION CRITERIA

Technical offers will be assessed separately against the evaluation criteria identified below. Point rated criteria not addressed in the Offeror's offer will result in a score of zero being assigned against that particular criterion.

Criteria Max. Available points Rating Scale Company

R1 For the five (5) projects listed under Mandatory Criterion M1 the Offeror should demonstrate if the referenced project included any of tasks I to VII listed in the Statement of Work, Section 5.0 Tasks.
30 points
The referenced project included:
0 points – none of the listed tasks
5 points – 1 of the listed tasks
10 points – 2 of the listed tasks
15 points – 3 of the listed tasks
19 points – 4 of the listed tasks
23 points – 5 of the listed tasks
27 points – 6 of the listed tasks
30 points – 7 of the listed tasks
Each project will be scored separately. The total number of points for each project will be summed and divided by five (5).
This is an easy way for the evaluator to determine a score. It is strictly number crunching against predeterminde criteria. For the bidder, it is an advantage and a disadvantage. It makes it equally easy for the bidder to ensure maximum points by itemizing how each of the tasks was done for each project. Conversely, it makes it equally easy for a competitor to obtain the necessary marks.

R2 For the five (5) projects listed under Mandatory Criterion M1, the Offeror should demonstrate how each project addressed each of the following elements:
• Improved client satisfaction
• Increased innovation in service delivery
• Reduced delays, lead times, inventories and costs
• Eliminated waste and focused on value-added activities
• Improved quality, productivity and capacity
15 points

Appendix C – Case Study

The referenced project addressed:
0 points – none of the listed elements
4 points – 1 of the listed elements
7 points – 2 of the listed elements
10 points – 3 of the listed elements
13 points – 4 of the listed elements
15 points – 5 of the listed elements
Each project will be scored separately. The total number of points for each project will be summed and divided by five (5).
This is similar to R1. Provided the bidder has listed five projects, by carefully writing an answer for each element for each project, a bidder should be able to obtain full marks.

R3 The Offeror should demonstrate experience with additional projects, over and above the five (5) projects listed under Mandatory Criterion M1, where the Offeror has provided process
8 points
The Offeror demonstrated experience with:
0 points – no other projects aside from the five (5) listed under Mandatory Criterion M1 were provided improvement services. For the purposes of this criterion, the Offeror did not have to hold the role of the primary contractor in the additional projects listed. Experience in a joint venture or as a subcontractor will be accepted.
2 points – 6 projects within 10 years from the date of bid submission
4 points – 7 projects within 10 years from the date of bid submission
6 points – 8 projects within 10 years from the date of bid submission
8 points – 9 projects within 10 years from the date of bid submission
This is unusual. Most RFPS do not allow work as a subcontractor to be counted. The customer is giving extensive weight to experience. This reduces the number of potential

bidders. *The evaluation process is easier if there few bids to evaluate.*

R4 Client contacts referenced at Mandatory Criterion M1 will be asked to rate the Offeror's overall performance on the project and the degree to which the client was satisfied with the work completed or completed to date. The overall performance will be based on the following aspects:
- quality of work
- process improvement methodology
- change implemented/recommended
- resource allocation

Referenced clients contacts will be asked the following questions:
24 Points

1. How would you rate your overall satisfaction with the Offeror's approach to reach a solution?
3 Points - Very Good
2 Points – Good
1 Point – Weak
0 Points - Poor or No Response

2. How would you rate your overall satisfaction with the Offeror's process improvement methodology?
(customer boilerplate not shown)

3. How would you rate your overall satisfaction with the results of the implemented changes, or the recommended changes, if not implemented, or not yet implemented?
(customer boilerplate not shown)

Each reference will be scored separately. The total number of points for each reference will be
summed and divided by five (5).

4. How would you rate your overall satisfaction with the Offeror's ability to allocate proper or sufficient number of resources to the project?
(customer boilerplate not shown)

Appendix C – Case Study

5. How would you rate your overall satisfaction with the Offeror's ability to meet pre-established schedules and objectives?
(customer boilerplate not shown)
6. How would you rate the Offeror's ability to ask prompting question in order to determine the source of task(s), seek a core understanding of the process and expedite/ensure the progression of process improvement?
(customer boilerplate not shown)
7. Did the methodology used help you identify any of the following: activity based costing, assigning level of effort, assigning risk, etc.
(customer boilerplate not shown)
8. Were you invoiced for any charges that you had not agreed to in the Contract?
(customer boilerplate not shown)
The evaluation grid is not too complicated, with only four possible responses. There will be some confusion between the definition of "weak" and "poor". The "no" response for zero points is of major concern as it could be unfair if the reason for no response was the inability to contact the reference.

Resources
R5 The Offeror should demonstrate ability to provide more than the three (3) resources required as a minimum as per Mandatory Criterion M2 – each with experience in a minimum of three (3) risk management improvement projects. A resume of each additional resource must be submitted with the offer in order to evaluate this criterion.
21 points
The Offeror demonstrates having:
0 points – no additional resources above the 3 mandatory resources
7 points – 1 to 3 additional resources above the 3 mandatory resources
12 points – 4 to 6 additional resources above the 3 mandatory resources

17 points – 7 to 9 additional resources above the 3 mandatory resources

21 points – 10 or more additional resources above the 3 mandatory resources

Note the importance attached to the resumes. This is where it becomes critical to ensure that information is complete in the resumes. As mentioned in this book, to ensure that information is not overlooked, an attachment can be made to each resume (which becomes part of the resume) to ensure that all information is complete. Also, you can gain significant competitive advantage by having additional people to do the work. The 10 specified here is in addition to the 3 specified in M2.

R6 For the resources listed in response to Mandatory Criterion M2, the Offeror should identify the resources' experience with the following:
• Facilitating interactive sessions to determine current state and identifying possible solutions
• Facilitating development of future state process maps
• Developing migration strategies from current state to future state
• Successfully implementing new process
• Providing coaching to clients' staff on process improvement
• Providing recommendations around change management
• Using process improvement methodology to identify level of effort and activity based costing

28 points
The proposed resources have experience with:
0 points – none of the listed elements
4 points – 1 of the listed elements
8 points – 2 of the listed elements
12 points – 3 of the listed elements
16 points – 4 of the listed elements
20 points – 5 of the listed elements
24 points – 6 of the listed elements

Appendix C – Case Study

28 points – 7 of the listed elements
Each resource will be scored separately. The total number of points for each resource will be summed and divided by the total number of proposed resources.

This criteria presents a problem for a bidder. The statement in M2 was a minimum of three (3) people. R5 was clearer asking for information on resources above the three minimum. At M2, for example, you may have offered six people with the expectation that at least three would qualify (the minimum). Now R6 states these additional three are going to be rated. The total may suffer as not all of the six can do the seven elements and they are averaged. On the other hand, a firm who offered only three and who can do all the elements would be awarded a higher mark. This appears unfair. More resources available should equal more points awarded, not less. Also, if three of your personnel (out of six) offered in M2 can do all the elements, it would appear that you should be awarded full marks. This is definitely in need of clarification through one or more written questions.

R7 For the resources listed in response to Mandatory Criterion M2, the Offeror should identify any education possessed by the resources above the minimum mandatory education at Mandatory Criterion M3.

Copies of diplomas and degrees, as applicable, should be submitted with the Offeror's offer. The DSQ will accept and recognize any foreign educational credentials as long as they are considered acceptable by at least one of the following: a Canadian educational institution, the International Credential Assessment Service of Canada (or similar and equivalent organization).

15 points
The resources proposed at Mandatory Criterion M2 possess:
2 points – multiple college diplomas
5 points – a college diploma in addition to an Undergraduate degree

7 points – multiple Undergraduate degrees
10 points – a Graduate degree
13 points – a Master's degree
15 points – a Doctoral degree
Each resource will be scored separately. The scores obtained by the 3 resources will be summed and averaged to obtain a total score for this criterion.

This is clearer than R6. They are evaluating the three resources from M1. However, there is still a question. Why is there a different score for Graduate degree (10 points) and Master's degree (13 points). This is a question worth asking.

Total Available Points   150 Pts
Minimum Points Required   105 Pts
*This illustrates the importance of checking all the information, including the weight factors given. If you add up the total points available (R1 to R7) the total is 141. There are 9 points not accounted for. 105/150 points results in a pass mark of 70%. 105/141 is a pass of 74.4%. At 2.2 above, it was stated, "Any offer that does not achieve an overall minimum score of **70%** will be considered noncompliant and will receive no further consideration." This earlier statement provides an indication that there is either a missing evaluation element or the weights assigned may be incorrect. To clarify this, the discrepancy in the RFP between the totals of 141 and 150 marks should be sent in a question to the customer.*

SECTION V – FINANCIAL OFFER

1.0 CEILING PER DIEM RATES

Offerors must quote ceiling per diem rates in Canadian funds, GST or HST extra as applicable for each year of the three year period of the Supply Arrangement.
The Canadian Price Index (CPI) will be utilized to calculate a rate for each option period as follows:

Appendix C – Case Study

First Option Period Rate = Third Year Rate of the Supply Arrangement + CPI
Second Option Period Rate = First Option Period Rate + CPI
Third Option Period Rate = Second Option Period Rate + CPI
(customer boilerplate not shown)

Financial Offers will be evaluated as follows:
TABLE V.1 – Supply Arrangement Period
Ceiling Per Diem Rate – Year 1 **(A)** $_____
Ceiling Per Diem Rate – Year 2 **(B)** $_____
Ceiling Per Diem Rate – Year 3 **(C)** $_____
TABLE V.2 Supply Arrangement Option Periods
Ceiling Per Diem Rate – Option Year 1 **(D)** $ (C) + CPI
Ceiling Per Diem Rate – Option Year 2 **(E)** $ (D) + CPI
Ceiling Per Diem Rate – Option Year 3 **(F)** $ (E) + CPI

This is simple to understand and well presented. You can follow exactly how your per diem maximum price will be allowed to change over six years.

The offer evaluation price will be derived by summing the ceiling per diem rates of years one (1) through (3) of the Supply Arrangement Period (Table V.1).

This is a very simple but common calculation when the amount of services are unknown. The evaluators simply sum the three per diem rates (A+B+C) and that becomes the financial calculation used in the proposal evaluation. While simple, this method is subject to abuse. Firms that knows the work and which professional level of the categories will be needed can, and often do, lowball pricing in the categories that will not be used. The risk is minimal since it is the category is not expected to be where the work is done. On the other hand, the rewards are great since the low price can dramatically lower the total evaluated price, resulting in winning the contract.

ANNEX A-1 TO PART 1: CERTIFICATIONS REQUIRED TO BE SUBMITTED AT TIME OF RFSA CLOSING DATE

1.0 TERMS AND CONDITIONS
(customer boilerplate not shown)
2.0 CONFLICT OF INTEREST
(customer boilerplate not shown)
3.0 EDUCATION AND EXPERIENCE
(customer boilerplate not shown)
4.0 LANGUAGE CAPABILITY
(customer boilerplate not shown)
5.0 CONFIDENTIALITY
(customer boilerplate not shown)
6.0 CERTIFICATION STATEMENT
(customer boilerplate not shown)

ANNEX A-2 TO PART 1: CERTIFICATIONS REQUIRED TO BE SUBMITTED PRIOR TO SA AWARD

1.0 FORMER PUBLIC SERVANT CERTIFICATION
(customer boilerplate not shown)
2.0 FEDERAL CONTRACTORS PROGRAM FOR EMPLOYMENT EQUITY - $200,000 OR MORE
(customer boilerplate not shown)

Part "2" - Model Supply Arrangement

SECTION I - GENERAL INFORMATION

1.0 DEFINITIONS
(customer boilerplate not shown)
2.0 SUPPLY ARRANGEMENT
(customer boilerplate not shown)
3.0 SERVICES COVERED UNDER THIS SA
(customer boilerplate not shown)
4.0 PERIOD OF THE SUPPLY ARRANGEMENT
(customer boilerplate not shown)

Appendix C – Case Study

5.0 OPTION TO EXTEND SUPPLY ARRANGEMENT
(customer boilerplate not shown)
6.0 PERIOD OF SERVICES OF THE CONTRACTS AWARDED UNDER THE SUPPLY ARRANGEMENT
(customer boilerplate not shown)
7.0 ESTIMATED EXPENDITURE AND QUANTITY
(customer boilerplate not shown)
8.0 NOTIFICATION OF WITHDRAWAL FROM THE SUPPLY ARRANGEMENT
(customer boilerplate not shown)
9.0 OFFICIAL LANGUAGES
(customer boilerplate not shown)
10.0 MANAGEMENT OF SUPPLY ARRANGEMENT HOLDERS LIST AND SUPPLY ARRANGEMENTS
(customer boilerplate not shown)
11.0 AUTHORITIES
(customer boilerplate not shown)
12.0 CONFLICTS OF INTEREST
(customer boilerplate not shown)

SECTION II STATEMENT OF WORK (SOW)
This section has been deleted as it is not required for the purposes of the RFP case study. In the case of an actual RFP, the SOW should be examined for completeness and inadvertent bias. Often, a specification or condition is contained in a SOW that only one firm or very few firms can do. The SOW may also inadvertently eliminate alternate methods of accomplishing the same goal. Finally, the SOW has to be compared to the evaluation criteria for consistency. It is not unusual for the evaluation criteria to be assessing something that has nothing to do with the work being requested.

1.0 TITLE
Risk Management Services

2.0 OBJECTIVE
3.0 BACKGROUND
4.0 SCOPE
5.0 TASKS
6.0 DELIVERABLES
7.0 LANGUAGE CONSTRAINTS
8.0 CLIENT SUPPORT
9.0 TRAVEL AND LIVING
Annex "A" - DEFINITIONS

SECTION III SOLICITATIONS ISSUED AGAINST THE SUPPLY ARRANGEMENTS - STAGE 2

1.0 GENERAL
(customer boilerplate not shown)
2.0 AUTHORITY TO RAISE CONTRACTS AGAINST THE SUPPLY ARRANGEMENTS
(customer boilerplate not shown)

3.0 SOURCING METHODOLOGY UNDER THE SA
a) For requirements estimated to be equal to or less than $25,000.00 (GST/HST included)
Contracting Authorities may select any one of the SA Holders.
b) For requirements estimated at over $25,000.00 (GST/HST included)
Contracting Authorities will use one of the following selection methods, either:
i) select the SA Holder using the cascade methodology, where the first ranked SA Holder
shall be given first consideration, should that SA Holder be deemed unable to carry out
the proposed services within the required time frame, the second ranked SA Holder will
be approached and so forth. The Contracting Authority must also document the reason

Appendix C – Case Study

why a SA Holder is not available or unavailable to perform the work; or
ii) compete among all SA Holders.

The above illustrates the complexity faced when there is an actual requirement. For requirements under $25,000 there is the danger of potential favouritism as the same supplier could be chosen every time. For requirements over $25,000 there is also the danger of favouritism. As written, the customer could, at their sole discretion, always use the number one ranked SA holder instead of competing among the five winners. This should be questioned and clarified.

4.0 PROCEDURES REGARDING REQUEST FOR PROPOSALS (RFP)

This is the procedure to be used when the requirement is competed among the five SA holders. As earlier stated, a RFP process will be used. Much of the information which give details has been deleted as it is not relevant to the analysis. What you now have is a process within a process. The first RFP process narrows the bidding possibilities to a maximum of five firms. The second RFP process is within the Supply Arrangements and limited to the five firms.

Step 1 - Statement of Work (SOW) The first step is to determine the requirement and prepare a SOW for a specific work requirement.
(customer boilerplate not shown)

Step 2 - Evaluation Criteria
The evaluation criteria shall be delineated in the RFP and their relative importance shall be stipulated.
(customer boilerplate not shown)

a) Mandatory Evaluation Criteria
Mandatory evaluation criteria identify at the outset the minimum requirements for bids to be
considered.
(customer boilerplate not shown)

Proposed Personnel Experience
The proposal must demonstrate that the proposed personnel meet the minimum experience requirements detailed in the RFP.
(customer boilerplate not shown)

b) Point Rated Evaluation Criteria
The RFP shall clearly state all evaluation factors and their relative importance.
(customer boilerplate not shown)
 The following are the categories that are to be used in the RFP.
Approach and Methodology
Understanding of the requirement
Experience and Expertise of the Firm
Experience and Expertise of the Proposed Resources
Experience and Expertise of the Proposed Resources
This reference is not to this bid that is being evaluated. As earlier described, the winner of the first bid, the RFSA, wins the right to bid on a competitive process (a RFP) when there is an actual requirement.

Step 3 - Basis of Selection
One of the following bases of selection will be identified in each RFP and will be used for selecting the contractor for each competed requirement:

a) Lowest Priced Compliant Proposal
(customer boilerplate not shown)

b) Best Value
(customer boilerplate not shown)

 (c) Lowest cost-per-point
(customer boilerplate not shown)

 (c) Highest Combination of Technical and Price Scores
(customer boilerplate not shown)

Step 4 - Basis of Payment (required for directed and competed requirements)
(customer boilerplate not shown)

a) Firm Price (FP) Contract: The FP contract includes reasonably well-defined requirements.
(customer boilerplate not shown)

Appendix C – Case Study

b) Fixed Time Rate Contracts (FTR):
(customer boilerplate not shown)

Step 5 – Issuing a Request for Proposal (RFP) against the Supply Arrangement
(customer boilerplate not shown)

Step 6 – Instructions for Submitting Proposals
Unless otherwise indicated in a specific RFP, the following "Instructions to Bidders" shall apply to all RFPs issued under this SA: In responding to the SA RFP solicitation, Bidders must provide their proposal in three (3) separate sections. The first section shall address the technical requirement and **one (1) original and three (3) copies** will be required by CRA. The second section will be the financial section, and only **one (1) copy** will be required. Bidders' proposals should be clear and concise addressing only the technical and financial requirements of the SA RFP. The third section will be the Certification section, and only **one (1) copy** will be required and the Bidder will need to sign all areas indicated within that section.
(customer boilerplate not shown)

It is important to realize that the normal RFP process is being described and that it is subsequent to the FRSA bid that you are developing your proposal for..

Step 7 - Evaluating of Proposals
(customer boilerplate not shown)

Step 8 - Contract Award
(customer boilerplate not shown)

Step 9 – Commencement of Work
(customer boilerplate not shown)

Step 10 - Debriefs (required for competed requirements)
(customer boilerplate not shown)

Step 11 – Financial Limitations
(customer boilerplate not shown)

SECTION IV RESULTING CONTRACT CLAUSES, TERMS AND CONDITIONS FOR STAGE 2 OF THE PROCUREMENT PROCESS

1.0 REVISION OF DEPARTAMENTAL NAME
(customer boilerplate not shown)
2.0 AGENCY RESTRUCTURING
(customer boilerplate not shown)
3.0 STANDARD CLAUSES AND CONDITIONS
(customer boilerplate not shown)
4.0 CONDITIONS
(customer boilerplate not shown)
5.0 PRIORITY OF DOCUMENTS
(customer boilerplate not shown)
6.0 REQUIREMENT
(customer boilerplate not shown)
7.0 PERIOD OF CONTRACT
(customer boilerplate not shown)
8.0 WORK LOCATION
(customer boilerplate not shown)
9.0 ACCESS TO FACILITIES AND EQUIPMENT
(customer boilerplate not shown)
10.0 IDENTIFICATION BADGE
(customer boilerplate not shown)
11.0 SITE REGULATIONS
(customer boilerplate not shown)
12.0 DELIVERY
(customer boilerplate not shown)
13.0 APPLICABLE LAWS
(customer boilerplate not shown)
14.0 BASIS OF PAYMENT
(customer boilerplate not shown)
15.0 TRAVEL AND LIVING EXPENSES
(customer boilerplate not shown)
16.0 LIMITATION OF EXPENDITURE
(customer boilerplate not shown)

Appendix C – Case Study

17.0 METHOD OF PAYMENT
(customer boilerplate not shown)
18.0 INVOICING INSTRUCTIONS
(customer boilerplate not shown)
19.0 T1204 – INVOICING INSTRUCTIONS
(customer boilerplate not shown)
20.0 INSURANCE REQUIREMENTS
(customer boilerplate not shown)
21.0 SECURITY REQUIREMENTS
(customer boilerplate not shown)
22.0 CONTRACTOR IDENTIFICATION PROTOCOL
(customer boilerplate not shown)
23.0 HANDLING OF PERSONAL INFORMATION
(customer boilerplate not shown)
24.0 TRAINING AND FAMILIARIZATION OF CONTRACTOR PERSONNEL
(customer boilerplate not shown)
25.0 FOREIGN NATIONALS (CANADIAN CONTRACTOR)
(customer boilerplate not shown)
26.0 FOREIGN NATIONALS (FOREIGN CONTRACTOR)
(customer boilerplate not shown)
27.0 ALTERNATIVE DISPUTE RESOLUTION
(customer boilerplate not shown)
28.0 AUTHORITIES
(customer boilerplate not shown)
29.0 CERTIFICATIONS
(customer boilerplate not shown)

ANNEX A CERTIFICATIONS TO BE PROVIDED AT TIME OF RFP CLOSING
(customer boilerplate not shown)
1.0 TERMS AND CONDITIONS
(customer boilerplate not shown)
2.0 STATUS AND AVAILABILITY OF RESOURCES
(customer boilerplate not shown)

3.0 CONFLICT OF INTEREST
(customer boilerplate not shown)
4.0 EDUCATION AND EXPERIENCE
(customer boilerplate not shown)
5.0 LANGUAGE CAPABILITY
(customer boilerplate not shown)
6.0 CERTIFICATION STATEMENT
(customer boilerplate not shown)

Appendix D – Template for Proposal Preparation
(created by Red Team as a guide for Proposal Team)

Example 1

Resources:
Note: This template is produced for M2. The mandatory criteria follows and is written in full as it appears in the RFP.

M2 The Offeror must demonstrate it has a minimum of three (3) resources – each with experience in a minimum of three (3) risk management improvement projects in the last five (5) years. The Offeror must provide a resume for all proposed resources, clearly demonstrating where, when and how experience in process improvement was obtained.

M2 Checklist
Has the following information been completed and provided for in the answer to Mandatory Criteria 2?

Resource 1 – Experience	Yes/No
Project 1 – Risk management improvement project	
Project 1 – when - within last five (5) years	
Project 1 – where experience was obtained	
Project 1 – how experience was obtained	
Project 2 – Risk management improvement project	
Project 2 – when - within last five (5) years	
Project 2 – where experience was obtained	
Project 2 – how experience was obtained	
Project 3 – Risk management improvement project	
Project 3 – when - within last five (5) years	
Project 3 – where experience was obtained	
Project 3 – how experience was obtained	

How to Respond to a RFP
Winning Proposal Writing

Resume attached	

Resource 2 – Experience	Yes/No
Project 1 – Risk management improvement project	
Project 1 – when - within last five (5) years	
Project 1 – where experience was obtained	
Project 1 – how experience was obtained	
Project 2 – Risk management improvement project	
Project 2 – when - within last five (5) years	
Project 2 – where experience was obtained	
Project 2 – how experience was obtained	
Project 3 – Risk management improvement project	
Project 3 – when - within last five (5) years	
Project 3 – where experience was obtained	
Project 3 – how experience was obtained	
Resume attached	

Resource 3 – Experience	Yes/No
Project 1 – Risk management improvement project	
Project 1 – when - within last five (5) years	
Project 1 – where experience was obtained	
Project 1 – how experience was obtained	
Project 2 – Risk management improvement project	
Project 2 – when - within last five (5) years	
Project 2 – where experience was obtained	
Project 2 – how experience was obtained	
Project 3 – Risk management improvement project	
Project 3 – when - within last five (5) years	
Project 3 – where experience was obtained	
Project 3 – how experience was obtained	
Resume attached	

Appendix D
Template for Proposal Preparation

Example 2

Note: This template is produced for R6 – Resources.. The rated evaluation criteria follows and is written in full as it appears in the RFP.

R6 For the resources listed in response to Mandatory Criterion M2, the Offeror should identify the resources' experience with the following:
• Facilitating interactive sessions to determine current state and identifying possible solutions
• Facilitating development of future state process maps
• Developing migration strategies from current state to future state
• Successfully implementing new process
• Providing coaching to clients' staff on process improvement
• Providing recommendations around change management
• Using process improvement methodology to identify level of effort and activity based costing

R6 Checklist

Has the following information been completed, demonstrated and provided for in the answer to Rated Evaluation Criteria R6?

Resource 1	Yes/No
Facilitating interactive sessions to determine current state and identifying possible solutions	
Facilitating development of future state process maps	
Developing migration strategies from current state to future state	
Successfully implementing new process	
Providing coaching to clients' staff on process improvement	
Providing recommendations around change management	
Using process improvement methodology to identify level of effort and activity based costing	

Resource 2	Yes/No
Facilitating interactive sessions to determine current state and identifying possible solutions	
Facilitating development of future state process maps	
Developing migration strategies from current state to future state	
Successfully implementing new process	
Providing coaching to clients' staff on process improvement	
Providing recommendations around change management	
Using process improvement methodology to identify level of effort and activity based costing	

Appendix D
Template for Proposal Preparation

Resource 3	Yes/No
Facilitating interactive sessions to determine current state and identifying possible solutions	
Facilitating development of future state process maps	
Developing migration strategies from current state to future state	
Successfully implementing new process	
Providing coaching to clients' staff on process improvement	
Providing recommendations around change management	
Using process improvement methodology to identify level of effort and activity based costing	

How to Respond to a RFP
Winning Proposal Writing

Appendix E
Professional Resume – Allan Cutler

Mr. Allan Cutler has over 30 years' experience in the public and private sector. During his career, he managed multi-million dollar complex and sensitive procurements being responsible for the successful evaluation, award and contract administration until the expiry of the contracts. He is skilled in troubleshooting with a demonstrated capacity to achieve results.

He has participated in developing Statements of Work and evaluation criteria for bid documents, which have been uniquely structured. He also assists firms in reviewing and in developing compliant proposals in response to competitive bid solicitations.

Allan Cutler also is a noted trainer and consultant in procurement and ethics. Presently he offers courses in Ethical Procurement, Negotiation Strategies, How to Respond to a Request for Proposal and Organizational Ethics. He is a frequent speaker on various ethical topics such as whistleblowing and organizational ethics.

Allan Cutler is also known as the "Whistleblower" from his involvement in trying to stop the abuses that resulted in the Sponsorship Scandal.

PRESENTATIONS

- Meeting Planners International, "Ethical Negotiation"
- Saskatchewan Crown Corporations, "Whistleblowing"
- 7th Annual Alliance for Excellence in Investigative and Forensic Accounting Conference, Whistleblowing

- The 8th Annual Ottawa Chapter Fraud Professionals' Conference, Whistleblowing
- Carleton University and St. Paul's University, "Whistleblowing and the Sponsorship Scandal".

TRAINING
- Ethical Procurement and Sustainability
- Negotiation Strategies
- How to Respond to an RFP
- Organizational Ethics

OTHER ACTIVITIES
- Advisor, Algonquin College, e-Business Supply Chain Management Advisory Committee
- Member, Materiel Management Institute
- Member, The Ethics Practitioner's Association of Canada
- Member, Transparency International
- President, Canadians for Accountability

AWARDS:
To The Top Canada Award, January, 2006. This is an award to recognize a Canadian who through their individual effort has made Canada a better place.

Five Who Made a Difference, January, 2006. The Ottawa Sun salutes Allan Cutler for making a difference to Ottawa "Government/Politics" in 2005.

One of the Top 50 People in Ottawa – 2005. Ottawa Life magazine

CONTACT INFORMATION:
Allan Cutler
E-mail: ascutler@ascutler.com

www.ingramcontent.com/pod-product-compliance
Ingram Content Group UK Ltd.
Pitfield, Milton Keynes, MK11 3LW, UK
UKHW041957230426
12048UKWH00008B/390